THE SACRED COW

By the same author

BLOOD ON THEIR HANDS:
The Killing of Ann Chapman

THE SACRED COW

*The folly of Europe's
food mountains*

RICHARD COTTRELL

GRAFTON BOOKS

A Division of the Collins Publishing Group

LONDON GLASGOW
TORONTO SYDNEY AUCKLAND

Grafton Books
A Division of the Collins Publishing Group
8 Grafton Street, London W1X 3LA

Published by Grafton Books 1987

British Library Cataloguing in Publication Data
Cottrell, Richard
The sacred cow : the folly of Europe's
food mountains.
1. Surplus agricultural commodities——
European Economic Community countries
I. Title
338.1'5   HD1920.5

ISBN 0-246-13224-8

Photoset by Deltatype Ellesmere Port
Printed in Great Britain by
Mackays of Chatham, Kent

For Tracy,
as always a marvellous comfort
and encouragement

CONTENTS

ACKNOWLEDGEMENTS

My grateful thanks are due in the first instance to my political assistant, Penny Craven, who has quarried much of the information in this book with patience, skill and imagination. My thanks also to my political colleague, David Curry, for help and guidance, particularly through the minefield of the EEC's agri-money system. Tony Gibson, the intelligent and capable secretary of Somerset NFU, contributed a number of provocative ideas and much useful background information on the state of the British industry. So has the National Farmers Union in London. Patricia Jamieson of Tate and Lyle was particularly helpful with the chapter on sugar. Although we rarely agree, I am grateful for the assistance of the Milk Marketing Board. In Brussels, Frank Wong of the New Zealand embassy and Brian Gardener of Agra-Europe were always at hand to deal patiently and kindly with complicated inquiries. Officials of the European Commission, too numerous to list at length, have been an unfailing help: but particular thanks are due to Peter Pooley, deputy director-general for agriculture. Professor Colin Spedding at Reading University and Professor David Grigg at Sheffield made important contributions: I could not have managed without statistical advice from Exeter University's department of agriculture. And in Ireland, Raymond Crotty contributed his own radical brand of thinking on farming and European matters in general. Staff at the Ministry of Agriculture in London

Acknowledgements

now know my name quite well. Consumer organisations in Brussels and London have been unfailingly helpful.

Richard Cottrell
Bristol
June 1987

INTRODUCTION

A Chronicle of Wasted Time

'Whom God would destroy He first makes mad.'

James Duport

The European Community celebrated the start of European Environment Year in 1986 by commissioning an adornment for a Brussels traffic roundabout costing £30,000. The worthy gastronomes of the EEC then took a satisfying 'symbolic walk' in a local park – after lunch of course. With meticulous timing – this was the 30th anniversary of the signing of the Treaty of Rome – the accounts department at the EEC had sent all Euro MPs a financial reckoning to mark the conclusion of three decades of work on the construction site of united Europe. This stated: 'The Community is at present faced with a budgetary situation which can only be characterised as being on the brink of bankruptcy.' In the United Kingdom, there were undignified scenes as elderly pensioners squabbled for a share of the butter mountain, a larger portion of which was being auctioned off to the Russians. Because of the impecunious state of the Community's finances, the EEC had no money of its own to facilitate this deal, and therefore passed the begging bowl to all twelve member states, issuing IOUs to be repaid in the uncertain future. Some butter, detained for so long it had turned rancid, had already been despatched to New Zealand for conversion into lipstick. An assiduous MEP had earned opprobrium by accusing the managers in

Brussels of directly fiddling the books, by disguising the true value (almost nothing) of the huge accumulations of unsold food stored all over Europe. At first strenuously denied, the charge was later admitted on all counts. On the EEC's birthday, 25th March 1987, the *Daily Telegraph* posed the imperious question: 'Does the Community exist for the fulfilment of its managers or the welfare of its citizens?'

It is nowadays hard to find anyone who really believes that a United States of Europe is just around the corner. This is not – as opinion polls commissioned by the EEC consistently stress – because the people of Europe themselves have lost faith in the idea. Even the British, traditional agnostics in the pantheon, are found to be touchingly attracted to the concept of a continent which truly reflects the joys of shared democracy. But they – in common with most other Europeans – no longer believe that the federal ideal can be sustained by the Tower of Babel which the European Community now resembles. At the end of thirty years, the EEC is synonymous with endless haggling over money – and the common agricultural policy. Yet the Treaty of Rome which founded the European Community was unequivocal in its ambitions: national frontiers would be swept away, the tonic of free enterprise and choice unleashed, all the artificial controls on trade and competition demolished. From such building blocks Europe would be assembled. Instead, practically all the cement has been used to construct the abiding folly of the CAP. Instead of breaking up and destroying cartels which suffocate trade and enterprise, the EEC is in a state of political paralysis imposed by an agricultural policy which has failed the people and broken the bank.

When I first went to the European Parliament after direct elections in 1979, I swiftly got into trouble by insisting that the EEC was on the road to ruin if it persisted in maintaining the common agricultural policy as an integral policy. Every development since then, each new twist and turn along the precipitous corniche, has proved me right. In 1987, farmers have been fined millions of pounds, for the sin of producing milk. Not potentially dangerous intoxicating alcohols, mind you, just milk. Dairy farmers have queued up to take their punishment rather than suffer what appears to be the worse fate of seeing the mattress provided by the common agricultural policy whipped away altogether. Economists observe that farmers have lost touch with the market place: consumers, who pay for the CAP, are disenchanted with mountains of excess which make Europeans seem smug and self-satisfied in a world of distorted food supply channels.

My attitude to agriculture has been compared by a colleague as rather similar to the prospect of letting Herod loose in a children's home. This is because I would, in a perfect EEC, sweep away all the stultifying ramifications of the CAP and let the stiff fresh breezes of competition and free enterprise blow vigorously through the world of farming. For this I am rebuked as a closet anti-European, privately stalking the collapse of the European ideal. These purblind critics contrive to miss the point: Europe's abiding commitment to the CAP has wrecked the hopes for a community which might stand comparison with the super powers. And that, after all, was the spirit which imbued the first signatures to the Treaty of Rome 30 years ago. This book is a chronicle of wasted time: but it is not too late for the Community to strike out with renewed courage and imagination for that prize which has slipped slowly from its grasp in the past three decades.

1

The Bitter Harvest

Dairy, prairie, quite contrary
How does your surplus grow?
With lobbies strong, so prices wrong,
And subsidies all in a row.

The Economist

The creation of the European Community always contained the essential elements of a biblical vision. The original architects of the Treaty of Rome chiselled their grand blueprint for a continent free from war, famine, plague and pestilence on the political equivalent of tablets of stone. In some European countries the dwindling band of enthusiasts who cling desperately to the fading dream of confederal union still refer to Hallstein, Schuman, Jean-Louis Rey and Sicco Mansholt as 'the founding fathers'. Belief in the founding fathers as political deities is alive and well in that vast antiseptic structure towering over the Brussels suburb which it dominates. Here are the teeming adherents of the grand post-war settlement, the toilers of the European Commission. One half expects, among the pot-plants, the dreary brown mock-Scandinavian furniture and stacks of paper, to encounter a posse of Italian *huissiers* scuttling along the corridors to attend matins at the shrine of the creators, clasping the Treaty and a copy of the staff regulations. No conversation inside the Berlaymont – a *'palais'*, by the way, in a strange invocation of which Kafka might approve – is complete without a solemn curtsy to

'The Treaty', of which dog-eared, well-thumbed copies may be found liberally distributed in every office. Visiting agnostics are frequently astonished by the ferocity with which even a mild questioning of the Holy Writ is repelled. The pan-European ideal still carries an enormous emotional charge among the 12,000-strong tribe who dwell in the Palais d'Berlaymont. To question is to doubt and the emergence of doubt sets at risk the theological basis of the tablets which the founding fathers handed down to the war-weary, dissipated peoples of Europe three decades ago.

Jonathan Swift once wrote that if any man could make two ears of corn sprout where only one had grown before, then such a man should enjoy the eternal thanks of all mankind. That of course was in the days of innocence before the common agricultural policy. The miraculous increase in farm productivity has bequeathed a monster which threatens to destroy the vision of a settled Europe, engulf the emergent community in a series of Orwellian campaigns against rival agricultural and trading powers and, eventually, disrupt the food supply system of the world. Dr Sicco Mansholt, who is Baron Frankenstein to his own man-made tyrant, never intended this to happen. Mansholt created the CAP as a foundation upon which the economic and social stability of Europe might rest. Instead, as political atrophy afflicted the great and original vision, the CAP was doomed to become the solitary keystone of Europe, whose removal might threaten the collapse of the entire political structure. By the early years of the 1980s it had become clear that the policy was economically intolerable yet politically indispensable. David Curry, a journalist who found his way from the sober columns of the *Financial Times* to the chairmanship of the European Parliament's agricultural committee, is fond of the analogy with the unfortunate sorcerer's apprentice. After he had uttered the words which set loose the spell of over-production on an unprecedented scale, no one could find the incantation to stop the nightmare. When the consumers of Europe buy food, they pay inflated prices guaranteed to spur the farmers on to ever-greater output. Politicians, always hungry for the rural vote and, in consequence, guilty of abject cowardice in the face of the vociferous farming lobby, refused to halt the giddy madness of the CAP – namely, abandon that most foolish promise to buy absolutely everything which the fields of plenty provide.

Farmers themselves have become remote from market pressures. As the great tide of subsidies swept over the land, they began to forget that agriculture is, by the laws of nature, an insecure and insincere master, subject to the harsh dictates of climate, demand and fickle public taste. In a sense the objective of the CAP was to raise a protective shield over the agricultural industry. When the Treaty of Rome was signed by the original six participant nations – Belgium, the Netherlands, France, West Germany, Italy and Luxembourg – in March 1957, about a quarter of the employed population of those countries owed their livelihood to the land. Many retained bitter memories of the pre-war recession and virtually all had further suffered from the privations of war itself. They demanded, and received, the most remarkable social pact achieved during modern history. This theme of total economic security still dominates contemporary thinking on the common agricultural policy. Michael Jopling, as Britain's minister for agriculture, has been fond of describing the problems of the CAP as those created by success. No one can doubt that the farmers kept their part of the bargain. Thirty years later, food production in Europe had swollen to totally unmanageable proportions, bequeathing a mountain of grain not far short of 17 million tonnes, just over one million of dried milk powder, some one and a half million tonnes of butter, 620,000 tonnes of beef and a small sea of 15,000,000 hectolitres of red wine, sufficient to entertain a regatta of cross-channel ferries. As Siberian winter swept down over Euope in the early months of 1987, the tabloid public prints in Britain revealed that 'EEC officials' had ordered the destruction of 23,000 tonnes of cauliflowers, which were then ploughed back into the very ground that produced them. The price of a cauliflower, now in artificial shortage, roared up to a pound apiece – all this the gift of a system designed in Brussels to protect Dutch horticultural co-operatives from the penalties of a glut. The bill for this single folly – paid by the European taxpayer – was £1.2 million. Even the *Farmers Weekly* in London was moved to denounce the episode, condemning it as 'morally wrong'.

Within days, Europe's farm ministers had endorsed a package conceived by the embattled European Commission to whittle down the beef and butter mountains with free hand-outs to those same chilled Europeans who had so recently been cheated of a plentiful supply of cheap vegetables. 'Beef bourgignon with the meals-on-wheels' was the sour reaction from Tony de Angeli, editor of the food trade magazine, the *Grocer*. And he added: 'But what about the needy who do not have meals-on-wheels, and don't go to OAP luncheon centres?' The scheme, which depended for mobility of distribution on voluntary charities in each member state, ran into predictable chaos. In Bristol, a con team posing as Salvation Army members tricked elderly victims out of their pension books with the false claim that they would return with the promised portion of the butter mountain. Because no effective supply lines had been established, greed instead of need compromised allocation of the Brussels manna. In my own constituency of Bath and Bristol, party officials had angry telephone calls from a residential centre for the elderly claiming that the 'Catholics up the road got twice as much as we did'. There were undignified squabbles, and even fights, at hand-out centres. Charity workers complained of being abused by irate pensioners. The beef, in fifty-kilo slabs, proved especially difficult to manage, since it required cooking and canning before distribution. Some genuinely needy people did get a pleasant surprise from Brussels, although few realised they had paid for this winter bonus many times over through the excessive taxes and additional food costs imposed by the CAP. The giveaway cost some £31 million, but the physical impact on the stockpiles was negligible. Even John Gummer, Michael Jopling's understudy at the ministry of agriculture, conceded that the scheme would make little difference beyond a nibble at the butter mountain.

Jopling himself looked uncomfortable with the entire enterprise, and at the opening of the International Food Exhibition in London had considerable difficulty maintaining enthusiasm for it while refusing to agree with puzzled questioners who thought the EEC should distribute 'social food' from excess stocks through a properly organised voucher system. The media wrote off the episode as more cosmetic engineering by the bureaucrats in Brussels. And while the pensioners queued up for their share at Salvation Army citadels throughout the land, the EEC was planning a new bargain-basement sale of butter and grain to the perpetually captive market of the Soviet Union. 'Reds get the giveaway butter,' screamed the *Daily Mirror*. And there were red faces, too, in the House of Commons, when the government was forced to admit it was lending £400 million to the bankrupt EEC so that Russians could buy butter at seven pence a pound.

It was also a mite unfortunate that officials in the agricultural directorate were in secret conclave with a delegation from New Zealand, the remit of which was to export some of the more antique butter stocks to the Antipodes for turning into lipstick and additives to diesel fuel. Since New Zealand is constantly under pressure to relinquish her political right to sell butter to Britain, the deal struck Brussels-watchers as especially piquant. The

Commission responded sniffily that the butter involved was mostly the salted variety which had long been a specialised British contribution to the stockpiles.

Such portents in the early days of 1987 confirmed the status of the CAP as a Greek tragedy, or a French farce. Roy Jenkins, former Labour minister and overlord of the European Commission from 1977 to '81 had, throughout his period in Brussels, proved a stout defender of the agricultural policy. I recall a prandial outing to an attractive Alsatian retreat (the wines were excellent) at which the President tried to convince a bunch of hearty doubters that selling cheap butter to the Russians was not such a bad idea after all. Jenkins declared again some years later that a break-up of the common market in food would threaten the survival of the Community itself. The member states should take concerted action to control the runaway costs of the CAP, or the pressure to impose solutions within their own frontiers – the so-called 're-nationalisation' of agriculture – would irreversibly weaken the political glue which held the Community together.

Ironically, it was while Roy Jenkins was behind the wheel in Brussels that the CAP juggernaut really ran out of control. Absolutely no one was prepared to slam on the brakes at the annual farm price fixing, a disgracefully bad-tempered affair where the participants deposit good manners and common sense at the door. The Commission always had good intentions of playing Cassius to Caesar. But it retreated in disorder year after year, once the Council – which has the real power and consists of the relevant minister from each country, each with his eye on home – began slashing to shreds any element of the Commission's package slightly tainted with price restraint. But price itself was never the complete answer. The only way to control the CAP, in terms of both cost and output, is to hack into the dense undergrowth of the intervention system, that sweeping forest of light-defying open-ended guarantees which is the core of the problem.

Beyond minor thinning at the fringes, nothing of substance was achieved.

Roy Jenkins has never really understood agriculture – the Chancellor of Oxford University could never be at home in a farmyard, picking his delicate way through the detritus of animal husbandry. The gestures match the mind – he is a man for all seasons of grand economic theory, hence his hypnotic attraction to the conception that reform of the CAP and completion of a genuine internal market could be achieved by a brave dash for economic and monetary union. The president therefore invested everything in creation of the European monetary system (EMS). But first James Callaghan and then Mrs Thatcher refused to pop sterling into this fancy new basket of Euro currencies. Once the door closed behind her at Downing Street, the new Tory premier laid down the law – the pound was in free float and would stay there. On top of which, she has always harboured a suspicion that committing sterling to the EMS would turn the Bank of England into the local branch of the Bundesbank. Legions of the good and worthy who try to convince her that this is nationalistic nonsense usually depart with red ears. Either way, monetary union is still no short cut to a dramatic shake-up of the CAP.

Right from the start, Thatcher had singled out 'getting my money back' – her euphemism for strapping down the size of the British contribution to the central community chest – as the number one political priority. This gory campaign preoccupied Community decision-making right through the early 1980s. Here was born the legend of Mrs Thatcher setting off for Brussels with a half-brick in her handbag, ready to clout obstinate opponents and bereft of any reluctance to start talking about money over the soup during bad-tempered dinners with her fellow Community leaders. Mrs Thatcher's determination to win them over to an elementary principle of natural justice sadly blinkered her normally canny instincts to the real grit in the system – the insatiable appetite of the common agricultural policy – itself the historic source of the 'British budget problem'. While the heads of state chewed the fat at a series of procrastinated summits, the Community cash-register hummed away in the background, notching up the over-spending on food and farming in terms of mega-millions. By 1987, agriculture was consuming two-thirds of a budget of £21 billion a year. And at that point, the money finally ran out, after Mrs Thatcher thought she had got hers back.

The Community had meanwhile embarked blithely upon the process known as 'enlargement', which means making the whole show bigger without doing anything to cure immediate and pressing problems afflicting the existing structure. Ireland, Denmark and Britain had joined the EEC on 1 January 1973. Now the born-again democracies of Greece (1981), Spain and Portugal (1985), were all shown the welcome mat without even momentary reflection on how to accommodate the prodigious appetites of yet more European farmers. Of course there were the usual haughty calls for fiscal rectitude. But as Roy Jenkins left Brussels to set sail for his new political career at the helm of the SDP, he left behind a community of nations bound straight for the rocks.

It is therefore not acceptable, as some commentators are wont to do, to lay the blame entirely on a 'cackle of vested interests, from the pocket handkerchief farmers of France, to the agricultural machinery manufacturers of Germany'. When he wrote that, Christopher Monkton, who formerly ranked as a policy adviser to Margaret Thatcher in Downing Street, had fundamentally misunderstood the origins of the CAP. For a start, the mini-farmers are thickest on the ground in Germany, where they are fiercely protected by ministers from the bikini party in the Bonn coalition, the Free Democrats. And as David Curry has pointedly observed, it is the Germans, not the French, who view farming, like gardening, as a sort of occupational therapy which helps to keep the Federal Republic tidy. And history has not been kind enough to a French socialist minister, Michel Rocard, who rushed into the EEC dairy with milk quotas, the first positive attempt to stem the flood of milk – a remarkable initiative which enraged the French farm lobby, hardly peaceful dissenters when they are suffering from only mild dyspepsia. Many are the British lorry drivers who can testify to hijacked cargoes of lamb, served up tarred and feathered in the streets. Rocard's immediate predecessor, Edith Cresson, suffered the indignity to her couture and person of being whisked by helicopter from the farmyard in Calvados where she was besieged by local *paysans* who were troubled simply by what the police described as 'general disorders' on that particular day.

The unstemmed policy drift in Brussels had left farmers all over Europe with a distinct feeling that the ground was moving uncomfortably beneath them. They lashed out predictably at Community bureaucrats, whom farmers' leaders branded for the 'politics of desertion' – a justified charge. And they also used their traditionally most effective weapon, the ballot box, against political leaders in their own countries. However, as the historic flight from the land began to accelerate, the vote looked like an increasingly blunt weapon, and nowhere more so than in the United Kingdom. The numbers game moved rapidly against the formerly all-powerful lobby. In 1939, there were 155,000 registered milk producers in the United Kingdom. Thirty thousand had gone by 1965. As the full impact of EEC agricultural policies hit the industry from 1974 onwards, flight turned into a headlong rush. There are now just 48,800 dairy farmers in the country, and over the next ten years, agricultural economists expect to see full-time farmers drop by some 30%. West Germany's farms, almost entirely small family operations, have halved in number since 1960 – down from 1,385,300 to just over 720,000.

The chart-makers in Brussels have been mostly pre-occupied with regulations designed to ease Europe's peasant farmers painlessly into the modern world. This conscious exercise is not only fatal to the small farmer – whom the Treaty was intended to protect – but has also proved distinctly dangerous to British farmers, who are mostly working larger acreages on an intensive scale with a high degree of mechanisation. Many have borrowed extensively to service the demand for higher output and to finance the upward spiral of land values, to the extent that the Agricultural Mortgage Corporation is now owed some £6 billion. The high street banks are also perched uncomfortably on a mountain of farm debt. Default, should it come, would reach Mexican proportions.

Europe's green revolution has therefore witnessed a stunning reduction in the political clout of farmers everywhere, a fact of which the present incumbent of the presidency of the National Farmers' Union, Simon Gourlay, is uncomfortably aware. Gourlay speaks of the sea change which has swept over the industry in the past five years. The reality of that change is reflected by the hostility which has replaced the traditional cosy relationship between the farmers' union and government even when the 'country party', the Tories, are in power. Gourlay received an unprecedented drubbing from Mrs Thatcher, who rained blows on his unfortunate head after the NFU conference in February 1987 gave Michael Jopling a miserable reception and went on to censure him for not defending the 'British interest' in Brussels with sufficient strength. The NFU leader was first roundly attacked by Mrs Thatcher in the Commons, on the grounds that no lobby group which lifted £2.5 billion from the taxpayer every year had any right to sound ungrateful; then Gourlay was ritually crucified at a meeting of the backbench Tory farming committee. In days not so long past, this would have proved dangerous heresy in the face of the landed interest, certain to earn revenge at the polls. Yet even Conservative MPs in relatively marginal seats have discovered a new balance between farmers who appear greedy for public money and increasingly sophisticated consumer opinion which cannot see why agriculture gets away with so much public subsidy. The farm lobby has run out of good tunes to hum. Singing about more when there is self-evidently too much already strikes a bad note. People do not think food is cheap, no matter how desperately one may try to convince them. And the unemployed – many of them evacuees from coal mines, shipyards and steel plants – cannot see why a tiny faction like the farmers appear to be special cases in perpetuity.

Before he left office, the former NFU president Richard Butler proved that he knew the old song so thoroughly that he could not face learning a new one. The maintenance of farming incomes remained a top priority for 'both rural economy and the common market itself'. In saying that he was of course repeating no more than Holy Writ as revealed in the Treaty of Rome. But the degree of unreality was reflected in this observation: 'One respects the Commission's desire to contain the budget but it is difficult to see how we move from where we are now to a better balance of supply and demand unless we have more money to do so.' And that of a budget which has already shot billions over the top. This is the authentic, unreconstructed ethic which has always dominated the farmers' view of the CAP. Butler's words were echoed by Ignaz Kiechle, West Germany's farm minister – who is to CAP reform what Stalin was to pluralist democracy – and François Guillaume, former head of the main French farming union transported by Jacques Chirac to the agricultural ministry. But in London, the new man at the NFU, Gourlay, has been retreating, telling all who seek his counsel that his members are not really after more money at all, only better value from what they already receive. 'We have no God-given right to limitless access to taxpayers' money,' he told me. If he sticks to that theme, Mrs Thatcher may offer him a sticking plaster next time.

All over Europe, agriculture has been receiving a host of confusing signals – emanating from Brussels, from their own national capitals, from the media and from the industry itself. The man who is theoretically in charge of the CAP is a quietly-spoken Dutchman, Frans Andriessen, who inherited the EEC's bed of nails from an undistinguished Dane. Andriessen had considerable difficulty coming to terms with his complex brief. He has a lawyer's mind for detail but not the grand sweep of policy. Without the leaden pressure of a budgetary crisis which has the capability to wreck the European Community, it is doubtful if Andriessen would have confronted the challenge. But he has proved transparently honest by admitting that the prospect of failure could already be detected in the Community's willingness to address the symptoms and not the disease. That disease the Agricultural Commissioner correctly identified as the guarantee to purchase food from farmers in unlimited quantities. He declares: 'Intervention in the market must return to its original role – as a safety net and not the standard outlet.' In many ways, Andriessen is a strange bird to roost where he does in the Berlaymont, like an ornithologist who develops a sudden taste for robbing nests. But he is sufficiently versed in liberal economics to distrust the global management of agriculture through heavy-handed bureaucratic regimes. The Commissioner surprised many by roundly condemning the prospect of taking land out of production by paying farmers to leave a part of their land fallow – which of course means that farmers would be paid to do nothing. 'If you make it compulsory, you will meet enormous resistance and run the risk of bureaucratising agriculture even more.' Hosannas of praise from all right-thinking, sensible people. But in the next breath, Andriessen announces that he wants a punitive tax on cheap vegetable oils to help unscramble the mess created by a vastly overheated oilseeds policy, which is just shorthand for more bureaucracy. The Commissioner does not look as though he is made of sound timber and this worries the carpenters. The formidable Kiechle has demanded and received Brussels money to experiment with 'set aside' in his beloved Bavaria. And even more alarmingly, the idea was strongly favoured by Britain's Michael Jopling and by Mrs Thatcher, who really should know better than to support a concept so completely at variance with her instinctive preference for the discipline of the market.

The Community's shameful food surpluses have without doubt overshadowed its wider and infinitely more significant political and economic ambitions. But control of over-production for its own sake has not been the crusading wisdom behind reform of the common agricultural policy. The shears were only brought out when financial ruin stared the European ideal in the face. The two options were therefore cutting the CAP down to size, or finding some other means to extract the cash from reluctant contributors. What the Community is now attempting is a confusing mixture of both. Thus, when the French president of the Commission, Jacques Delors, stepped down to the European Parliament in Strasbourg in February 1987 to unveil the long-awaited package of financial reforms, what he actually demonstrated was a three-card trick with the Community's existing resources, plus the added benefit of sleight of hand designed to provide the Commission with the effective power to raise its own taxes. For years the Commission, which sees itself as Europe's government-in-exile, has itched to get its hands on independent money-raising powers, putting an end to those unseemly wrangles like Mrs Thatcher's campaign to get her money back. Delors was at least honest enough to talk about this previously closely-guarded ambition in public. At the heart of these startling thoughts was a proposed levy on 'financial transactions' within the twelve member states. Delors, a doctrinaire French socialist who loves the Meccano-like structure of the EEC and the chance to bolt on bits and pieces and throw them away again, intended that part of his message should be received loud and clear in the City of London. The Paris bourse has never forgiven London for grabbing all that was worth having in the world's financial marketplace and regards the grubby capitalism conducted post-Big Bang with fastidious distaste. That became clear when Delors, adopting a seminary tone, peered over his pince-nez and declared with exquisite relish: 'When I think of the poor farmers in the Community, I think that 26-year-olds on high salaries should do their bit for Europe.' What we heard at Strasbourg was precious little about reform of the CAP – 'the shackling of the hydra', as the *Daily Telegraph* is often wont to call it – and too much about the Commission's own private political ambitions, all of it held together with a mixture-as-before sermon on greater European unity. Roy Jenkins might have been a great reformer but developed distracting illusions about music in the spheres such as the EMS: Delors has no revolutionary blood whatsoever coursing in his veins. One should mention that between these two, a little man from Luxembourg was in charge for a while, but no one now remembers him.

For the immediate future, then, it appears that more than 300 million people in Europe who are not farmers could go on forking out bloated taxes and inflated prices to sustain the CAP. The Delors package, sweetened as it was with promises of extra spending on user-friendly programmes like the regional policy, the social fund and scientific research, set alarm bells ringing in Whitehall because it appeared to threaten the perpetual British rebate won by Mrs Thatcher. But most of my colleagues trooped out of the chamber convinced that Delors, by demanding a larger if more orderly budget, had succeeded in swinging the propellers of European unity with sufficient vigour to get the craft airborne after a prolonged period in the hangar. Few paused to question the desirability of additional spending on structural schemes – such as pump-priming the regions with jobs at £75,000 apiece, and jacking up the input into top-heavy social engineering projects. And lamentably few detected the dragon's teeth in the Delors plan – like the independent tax-raising powers which would postpone to far distant horizons any prospect of effective parliamentary control over agricultural expenditure, a long-cherished yet always frustrated Strasbourg ambition.

In the days when the European Parliament functioned as your obedient servant to the farming lobby – and attempted to hike farm prices into stratospheric regions far beyond those contemplated in the Commission or the Council of Ministers – some justifiable suspicion attached to the motives of Euro MPs. Yet it is also true that the only effective policing of the common agricultural policy has been sponsored by individual MEPs who sit up late at night going over the books. Peter Price, Conservative spokesman on budget policy, openly accused the Commission of false accounting over the value of surplus foodstocks. Whilst refusing to reproduce their reckoning logic on paper, the bureaucrats insisted that the book value of the mountains of butter, beef and sugar, together with the lakes of wine and olive oil, should be put at £8.5 billion. The cost of stuffing coldstores and warehouses was estimated by Price at around £2.8 billion every year. Using average world prices as a guide, he concluded that the real value of the surpluses should be written down to no more than £2 billion. In other words, the storage costs exceeded the book value in a single year. Creative accountancy would be a polite description, but Price went further. 'Clearly everyone involved should be certified,' he declared. He found the Commission guilty of fiddling the balance sheets by refusing to depreciate the value of commodities held in store – which is of course a legal requirement in private enterprise. 'If you knowingly publish balance sheets which show certain assets at a certain value, when you know their true value is half or even less than half the value shown, then you are in trouble with the law.' Here was a charge that highly-paid officials in Brussels were authorising expenditure on storage of food – much of it decaying in quality by the day – far in excess of any realistic scale of value. The pity is that no one can summon the bailiffs to the doors of the Berlaymont. Theoretically, a separate institution – the mighty-sounding Court of Auditors – is charged with the responsibility of probing the Community's peculiar little ways with other people's money. But there are no tumbrils on the road to Luxembourg, since the court enjoys no sanctions it might employ to enforce compliance with its judgements. The European Parliament is everyone's Aunt Sally: yet many of its members have developed a tough and combative style in getting to grips with the follies of the CAP: if only the Parliament would stick to that instead of going on about cruelty to oysters and the healthy benefits of cycling.

When the hapless Michael Jopling went to the NFU annual conference in February 1987 to announce that the Conservative Party had been converted to the cause of agricultural reform (the only taker so far out of the EEC's twelve governments) he was so nonplussed by the hostile reaction that, as one major farming magazine cruelly observed, he forgot the name of a close friend with whom he once sat in conclave on the NFU's inner council. What he did not say was that the so-called dramatic gains of 16 December 1986 were already being eaten up by the CAP's unrequited appetite for money. This new round of draconian cuts imposed on milk and beef production in a series of pre-

Christmas political marathons in Brussels had already acquired a kind of mythical significance. This was because they had been achieved during the British 'presidency' of the EEC, in truth no more than an alphabetical turn on the carousel which confers six months behind the counter on each of the twelve member states. Extravagant hopes are always invested by individual powers who seek to leave behind their own indelible stamp on common market affairs. This looks particularly good if there happens to be an election around. Unfortunately, the Community's micro-powers, like Greece, Portugal and Ireland, are quite unable to provide anything like sufficient administrative back-up to fuel a serious presidency. Heads are still aching in Brussels after the first Greek run at the job. Britain's turn always suffers from the additional handicap of coinciding with August, which means a month lost through the annual political hibernation from which the Eurocrats refuse to be seduced. The British are also hampered by their irritating habit of concentrating on pragmatic issues like cheaper air fares or cutting down on paperwork for lorry drivers. This workmanlike approach butters few parsnips in Brussels, where the summit-managers have acquired a taste for swollen communiqués loaded with chatter about the march to European unity. And indeed, in those drear days of December the British presidency appeared embarrassingly short of anything which might be usefully recycled at home. At this point, Michael Jopling to the rescue. The *Daily Telegraph*, the least *communautaire* of all the British national dailies, fetched out unusually large slab type to record – 'EEC conquers the food mountains'. Sherpa Jopling came home confidently anticipating a festival of national rejoicing.

Since the reported savings achieved on 16 December 1986 were in the order of £800 million, and this in the deeply troubled milk and beef sectors alone, the claims of real progress on CAP reform made to the House of Commons appeared to possess genuine substance. But even as the twelve weary agricultural ministers prepared to depart into Christmas retreat, dangerous pressures were accumulating inside the combustion chambers of the European monetary system. By early January, they exploded, blowing sky high all the hard-won achievements of the past December. The relentless upward spiral of the German mark sent waves of depression over its associated currencies tagging along in the EMS. The subsequent realignment, presided over by the Belgian finance minister, in consequence created factional disorder among the EEC's ghostly 'green currencies' – the artificial exchange rates created at the insistence of the French and Germans to govern farm trade within the Community. These green rates are supposed to prevent West German farmers being showered with more pfennigs from heaven every time the mark hardens. So on 12 January, Herr Kiechle's social gardeners remained at standstill, but the rest of the Community's farmers received an attractive New Year's bonus of about 3%, the amount by which the Deutschmark had been revalued. The impact was to wipe out virtually all the cash savings of the great reforms, the ink on which was yet barely dry. To make matters worse, the price increase automatically triggered off a hike in the subsidies which are necessary to unload surplus food on the world market. No wonder *The Economist* moaned: 'Heads – the farmers win: tails – the Community loses.'

2

In The Beginning. . .

'The objectives of the common agricultural
policy shall be . . . to ensure a fair standard
of living for the agricultural community, in
particular by increasing the individual
earnings of persons employed in agriculture.'

– article 39, Treaty of Rome

Lost among the polders of north Holland, in the tiny village
of Wapserveen, stands an attractively restored 17th-
century farmhouse. There dwells in retirement the architect of the common agricultural policy, Dr Sicco Mansholt.
He is now 78, regarded by some as a genius whose
remarkable vision was debased by his successors, and by
less considerate critics as the one man who, more than any
other, should bear responsibility for the contemporary
afflictions of the European Community. When the former
Dutch farming minister and passionate lifelong socialist
went to Brussels, there to become the first EEC Commissioner for Agriculture, the wounds of the Second World
War had begun to heal. In the Europe of 1957, most of the
post-conflict shortages in the emotionally-crucial food
sector had already effectively vanished. In Britain, the last
vestiges of food rationing had been swept away by Winston
Churchill in 1954. All Europeans on the right side of the
Iron Curtain once again enjoyed a nutritionally stable, if not
luxurious, diet. The 'high contracting parties' who
gathered in Rome to sign the treaty establishing the

'European Economic Community' included the politically rehabilitated West Germans. The 'old fox', Konrad Adenauer, had escorted the democratic rump of the defeated German empire back into the company of respectable European democracies. In those heady days, there seemed no limits to what the infant Community might achieve. Percipient observers had already identified the Federal Republic as the nation most likely to succeed. Marshall Aid from the United States had applied balm to war-ravaged industry, laying the foundations of the post-war German economic miracle. NATO – the Pax Europa to which the British fervently contributed, while loftily refusing any closer embrace with the new European consensus – set in place the framework of security for the continent's democracies, backed by the Truman doctrine of political compact with Europe. It seemed that parties were continually in progress all across the Continent. But there was one, at Messina, the British refused to attend. Here the final brushwork was applied to the economic treaty conceived as the last major component of 'designer Europe'.

By refusing the invitation to Messina, Britain excluded herself from a seat at another much more important table in Rome, where the high contracting parties signed a treaty whose substantial elements remain virtually unchanged. The absent British stood accused of excessive nationalism, a charge regularly regurgitated whenever she tries to alter the geography agreed in Messina. The hangover still aches to this day whenever the subject of agriculture comes up.

The dream of Sicco Mansholt was a land fit for happy and prosperous farmers, toiling away in weather fair and foul yet still guaranteed a good rate for the job at the end of a long day. Beneath a canopy of standard prices for a wide range of products – finally erected in 1960 – farmers would receive the guaranteed income they were promised in the Treaty of Rome. This promise was not only generous, it was cast in the legislative equivalent of concrete. No one else in

Europe received such lavish treatment. It is the most precise and irresponsible example of automatic income indexation ever made in a binding treaty. Almost as an afterthought, a throwaway line attached to article 39 whispers of the need to ensure that 'supplies reach consumers at reasonable prices'. But unlike the specific contract made with the farmers, Mansholt and his fellow-architects failed to specify what kind of economic engineering they had in mind to ensure that consumers, too, received their fair deal and reasonable prices. To Mansholt, a fair price was that left over after the farmers had taken their bite. Consumers should be thankful for regularity of supply. In the Europe of the late 1950s, there was no such creature as a concerted and well-organised consumer lobby. Even now it exists only in tenuous form, compared to that 'cackle of vested interests' behind the CAP. What Mansholt laboured to create for European agriculture – a massive, inflexible combine harvester constructed from subsidies and guaranteed prices – would eventually collide head-on with the interests of consumers, who can only benefit when market forces are unleashed.

'My fear is that my dream of 30 years ago will be ruined if we go on as we are,' Mansholt declares now. He insists that no one in 1958 foresaw how the juggernaut of excessive production would crush his vision, drive farmers headlong from the land, invoke trade wars across the globe and threaten the very existence of the European Community itself. But even as the draughtsmen sculpted the outline features of the CAP, the beginnings of a new industrial revolution could be clearly discerned at work in the recuperating European economy. The Germans would enjoy this first, and harness that economic supremacy from which they have never been dislodged.

Yet it apparently occurred to no one – and certainly not the good Dr Mansholt – that science and technology could work the same kind of miracles in agriculture as they did with industry. Many of today's difficulties with over-supply are sponsored by research and scientific application of fresh knowledge to crops and animals. In the UK alone, the productivity of arable land has doubled in three decades, thanks largely to radical advances in crop strains and startling improvements in pesticides and fertilisers. Milk production per cow has gone up by 50% in 25 years. A new hormone, which several major companies would dearly like to market throughout the EEC – bovine soma-tatropine (BST) – can multiply the yield from a single cow by up to 40%. As the granaries bulge and a milk lake slops at the rims, there is still no limit to the ingenuity of laboratory farmers to breed more super-cows and wonder-wheat. Small wonder even Michael Jopling was forced to admit: 'To apply science in a constructive and co-ordinated manner, it is necessary to stand back and take a wider view.' Sufficiently far back, presumably, to avoid seeing any consumers, who in a rational world of agricultural management would benefit from such advances – lower costs, higher quality, fairer prices – instead of which every shopping basket carries its share of the dead weight of subsidy imposed by the CAP. When brooding on his fractured dream, Mansholt forgets that within one generation, and certainly two, from the foundation of a 'land fit for farmers', technology had built a high-speed by-pass around the fickle dictates of nature. Couple to that the intensive use of public subsidy as fertiliser and the social pact with farmers enshrined in article 39 of the Treaty of Rome, and the road leads straight to old-age pensioners squabbling over a sliver of the butter mountain.

The intellectual basis on which the CAP rests was already seriously in question before Mansholt even moved into his office in Brussels. By 1958, food production in free Europe had mostly returned to pre-war levels under the divergent systems the original Six practised independently before they threw everything into the new CAP. Even Germany –

which had lost most of its grain-producing territory to the east – was largely self-sufficient. At this point, a catastrophic decision was made, the full import of which would not be realised for twenty years. From the start of the negotiations which led to a regime of common pricing in 1960, the Germans insisted that support for farmers should be based on the inflated levels prevailing in the Federal Republic, compared with the very much lower incomes of French farmers. Even in these embryonic days of the EEC, Germany employed Prussian belligerence to get her way. The French, who thought this a fine ruse to jack up farm incomes at someone else's expense, acceded and in that moment, made the emergent Community a permanent hostage to the CAP. The French also seriously damaged their own long-term political interests inside the EEC, although they had no inkling of it at the time. At a stroke, they destroyed their potential agricultural primacy by surrendering their inbuilt advantages of low cost in-puts linked to an unusually favourable climate which can produce a cross-section of most temperate agricultural commodities of the highest quality. That British legion of unreconstructed Francophobes – most of whom cherish a peasant idyll of French agriculture which vanished years ago – are missing the point when they blame the French for the CAP. If emergent Europe had opted to harmonise from the start at French price levels, then the story would have turned out differently today. It was the Germans who fouled the system up by being greedy and the French simply took advantage of what looked like a heaven-sent opportunity. Scowling at these developments across the Channel, Britain played no part in the negotiations whatsoever. But from the moment the Six made this singular error, the engine of over-production had been – at the time, imperceptibly – switched on.

Peter Pooley is, in jovial Brussels parlance, a 'Brit' who has sat through many a Euro-marathon intended to squeeze the CAP back into the strait-jacket it so resolutely refuses to wear. He presides over his responsibilities as deputy director-general for agriculture with an air of elegant detachment which some of his continental compatriots mistake for profanity. Speaking at a major conference in London on the future of farm policy in February 1987, his topic was the great milk and beef shake-up the previous December. Official communiqués from the farm summits were never like this. 'There is no night, day, job, wife, love, hate, friend, house, dog – there is nothing but the negotiation . . . after the first three days of total lack of care and attention, most of us find it distracting that our bodies ache, creak, squeak, moan, gurgle, rumble and stink. A moment's distraction, one feels, or lapse of memory can cause disaster, like the whole of the Cumbrian flock of Herdwick sheep falling, splish splash, into a juridical void.' But Mr Pooley is equally elegaic in his defence of the conventional wisdom of the CAP. He concedes that by the late 1950s, production itself should not have been the incentive. Rather, the Community should have been aiming at unifying an important economic bloc, with agriculture as just another part of the deal. 'That's what the EEC is supposed to be about. But now, if you threaten to take away the CAP, the screams can be heard all the way to the thirteenth floor' (sometimes known as the roof garden, the administrative penthouse where the 17 Commissioners of the EEC reign over their empire). Pooley preaches that the Mansholt vision was essentially related to a largely pre-war world, in which people felt emotionally attached to farmers and the land – 'horny-handed sons of the soil they could see when they drove to work every day at Fiat or IBM, just as long as it wasn't actually them who had to do any grubbing about in the fields.'

The failure to evolve the Community beyond one common strategy – the CAP – left no alternative but to hang on to what had been achieved and hope for a bit more in the future. In his office in Brussels, Pooley mused: 'The absence of a CAP or something like it would appear to suggest that no common pricing of agricultural commodities could exist. If the Germans paid more for butter, then all the butter in Europe would shoot off to intervention in Germany. So Bonn would slap on border controls and taxes, then the common market in food products would fall apart and everything else would follow. That is the dreadful yawning chasm which no one wants to contemplate.' Even if one is taking a long view of European unity there is a disturbing lack of economic theory to support that argument. But Pooley does admit that the CAP has 'lost all credibility in the eyes of consumers, taxpayers and voters and unless that credibility is restored, the whole enterprise will founder for lack of the financial means to support it'.

The house that Mansholt built was a rigid protectionist structure inside which European farmers could shelter from cheap imports on the world market. He had no doubt they would all go bankrupt if the new-born EEC opened its doors to a flood of imports from all and sundry, and then consumers would face food shortages. There never was a shred of evidence to support such a fallacy. But amid the intoxicating atmosphere which prevailed on the post-war building site where the new Europe was under construction, it seemed reasonable to assume that rapid economic progress would be made on parallel fronts apart from agriculture. A system of common prices for farmer and producer, albeit rigged against the latter, would eventually have to be plugged into a single common market in everything. There was much fanciful discussion of 'fusing' the individual component economies together – the process known as 'convergence'. This is still a hallowed word in Brussels, despite the obvious difficulties of 'converging' the economies of Greece and Germany, let alone those of Britain and France, or even approximating the weird internal economic chemistry of Italy. It all suggests adventure on a truly heroic scale which might be compared not unfairly with the search for the Holy Grail.

As the European economy gathered speed, the Germans in any case roared out of sight, powered by their private version of the economic miracle. Serious tensions were also erupting inside the CAP, already straining to burst the artificial restraints created by Mansholt. Although the Community was hitched firmly to the German farm-price wagon, every time the Deutschmark hardened, it made nonsense of the vision of common prices. All the other farmers in Europe were getting cold while the Germans roasted at the fireside. The fatal weakness in the system was that Mansholt believed he could achieve common pricing without a single unitary currency. So the decision was reluctantly taken to knock out one of the major pillars in the Mansholt design – the idea that a common market in farm prices could exist without an array of crutches to keep the patient upright. The French wanted more 'protection' inside the already fiercely protected zone of the CAP. The Italians and the Belgians also endorsed the concept of a buffer system which would iron out discrepancies between the various currencies. So the 'green currencies' were born, conceived as a temporary expedient until such time as the member states reached the fabled land of monetary union. Temporary solutions have a way of becoming permanent in the machinations of the EEC and so it was with the green currency arrangements. As each new member state stepped over the welcome mat in Brussels, they received a pack of green Monopoly money to enter the CAP game – Britain juggles with five green pounds, each for a different product – together with their political credentials. Thus it is that the value of the 'green pound' is an issue of pre-eminent fascination for the NFU and their compatriot unions among the other eleven member states. It is a remarkable experience to hear Wiltshire farmers burring away about the latest gyrations of the green pound while downing pints of winter warmer after the local branch meeting.

But the new system, deceptively brilliant in conception, soon had everyone at each other's throats again. There was much special pleading every time one country felt it was getting a raw deal. 'Me too', or more appropriately, 'me first', politics are constantly bubbling just beneath the surface of the EEC. Once they joined the club, the Irish, burdened by a chronically-weak currency, made a speciality of demanding privileged revaluations of the 'green punt', provoking predictable uproar from the British. Since all agreements within the Community are a lethal cocktail blended from horse-trading, blackmail and bribery, it becomes imperative for even one delegation isolated on a single issue to stick out to the very last, so that in the end, exhausted participants can only get home to shave and sleep by giving in. Games of 'Euro Monopoly', played around the clock (and sometimes with the clocks actually stopped, so that time effectively stands still) are hugely exploitable opportunities for displays of the nationalistic selfishness which are the abiding characteristic of the EEC. It is yet to be proved whether the recent treaty adjustments will civilise the process.

The green currencies thus introduced new elements into this already discredited game. The not-so-funny money invented in Brussels proved capable of strange alchemy. It can turn a swingeing cut in farm support prices into an actual increase, an unforeseen side-effect which makes nonsense of common pricing – Mansholt's dream – and means, to give but one illustration, that the already super-upholstered German farmer gets paid £150 for a tonne of wheat or barley, and the same man harvesting the East Anglian prairies with equal toil, just £112. In 1969 – once again for short-term political expediency – another terrifying dose of complexity was injected into the system. Enter 'monetary compensation amounts'. These are, in effect, border taxes, which ought no more to exist in the EEC than satanic regalia in a cathedral. There were troubles again on the Franco-German border. The French were making a lot of money dumping cheap food in high-cost Germany and upsetting German farmers no end. In a world where temporary always means 'for ever', MCAs soon acquired a fixed position in the EEC firmament. Killing them off again required more political courage than anyone had because the system could be manipulated to stop farmers in weak-currency countries (Italy, the UK, et al) making big profits by selling in rock-hard money markets like Germany, thus deflating the prices and profits the German government preserves with single-minded determination. Governments could rig the system so that one man's price cut is another man's price rise. In 1971, as a reflex to the disorder which the oil crisis induced in the world's money markets, MCAs were rendered flexible or, in Euro-jargon, 'variable'. Another major plank was hoisted into the already groaning stack of Euro money in the form of a green equivalent of the unit of account, a blend of all twelve member states' currencies which the institutions of the EEC use to do all their internal sums. A senior official of the Commission, whose miserable burden it is to make daily sense of this financial maze, confided to me glumly: 'What we do here is exceedingly difficult and complex. The Community is operating a method of accounting in which two and two make five, and ten-plus-three equals zero. A visitor from another planet would think the zombies had taken over. And all this, mind you, to run the farmyard.'

By 1968 even Mansholt conceded that his cherished vision had gone appallingly astray. He therefore proposed dramatic reforms intended to cut to the heart of the problem, that too many farmers were already producing too much food. Mansholt is of course a structuralist: if this one fails, get out the drawing board and run up another one. He did precisely that and came up with CAP mark two. The kindly and well-meaning Mansholt was shocked

41

beyond compare by the abuse then heaped upon his head. One German newspaper thundered: 'This man should be killed.' This to a modest wartime hero in the Dutch resistance. Mansholt's crime was to suggest that Europe had grown a surplus of farmers and their numbers should be drastically thinned – from around ten million at that time, to five million. This would be achieved by social payments to get the small men off the land and a whole new range of incentives designed to achieve a leaner, fitter European agriculture. Farmers would also be paid to take marginal farmland out of production completely (a theme which exercises a strange fascination for Mansholt to this day). But no one wanted to listen, and certainly not the rich Germans. In Bavaria, the feudal overlord Franz-Josef Strauss warned that not so much as a blade of grass would be touched by Mansholt's fearful new scheme. Strauss, of course, was interested only in the survival of that protected species, the five-cow Bavarian farmer. Years later, in retirement in Wapserveen, Mansholt muses bitterly that in the late 1960s the vital chance of reform was missed through political cowardice. In fact, CAP mark two was no better than the first: Mansholt could not bring himself to take the axe to subsidy.

When the time came to fit British agriculture into the European jigsaw, political convenience entirely subsumed the detail of the argument. The Foreign Office, preoccupied as always by grand designs and desperate to get aboard the European lifeboat at any cost, wrote off agriculture as a wretched diversion from the real business, that of consigning such distractions as empire and commonwealth to the margins of history. When Edward Heath went off to Paris to win the support of the hostile French, President Pompidou told him bluntly that the British must buckle down to the CAP and sever their trading links with the Commonwealth, or they could fold their tents and remain

Europe's offshore island for ever. Pompidou then went on television to declare that he had wrung this humiliating contract from Heath before agreeing to lift the French veto on British membership. British agriculture therefore embarked upon its most dramatic transformation since enclosure and reform of the Corn Laws. It is true, as David Curry argues, that the British had been digging enthusiastically for victory since 1939. 'We were into the gut spirit of production,' he says, 'every bit as much as the French.' Farmers received millions in aid every year, eagerly anticipating the annual price review to judge the scale of their continuing reward.

But there was one essential difference between British largesse and how matters were arranged across the Channel. The British used a costly preference system which amounted to direct income support. Just like the CAP, it cost the consumer dear, but had the one attractive advantage of avoiding the automatic generation of surpluses. We had also permitted generous imports from the Commonwealth – meat and butter from New Zealand, wheat from Canada, Caribbean sugar, cheese and fruit from Australia. The effect of this was to maintain prices somewhere near the world level, to the considerable benefit of the consumer. Such a delicate balancing act between widespread state investment in agriculture, coupled with an open door to the Commonwealth in particular, became known as the 'cheap food policy', to which post-war governments of all persuasions remained firmly wedded. Until, that is, Edward Heath hustled a still-reluctant country into the common market.

Sir Richard Body, who is a withering critic of the CAP and chairman of the Commons select committee on agriculture, says that ever since, farmers have been disappearing off the land at a rate unequalled since the Black Death. He goes on to cite other attendant misfortunes, like 125,000 miles of hedgerow lost before the advancing plough, millions of acres of ancient woodland and cherished moor and heath sacrificed to the treadmill of over-production. Farmland is drenched with chemicals, pesticides and fertilisers, all designed to invert nature, to the point where nitrate levels of some watercourses now exceed the margins considered safe by the World Health Organisation. Body believes that the farmers' role as a steward of the countryside may be gone forever – or at least until intensive farming is brought to an end, and even then, he thinks it may take the land half a century to recover. Sir Richard calculates that since the Second World War, some £70,000 million has been pumped into agriculture by willing governments, a bounty which averages out at around £250,000 for each farm. The old pre-CAP support structure was hardly cheap. It still meant that around 70% of a farmer's income came from the wage-packets of the taxpayer. Under the CAP, that figure has shot up to over a hundred per cent, and that, says Body, is 'farming in the clouds'. His view that farmers have become addicted to intraveneously-injected money won him few friends among the grandees of the NFU: no matter, he simply went off and formed his own union, aimed mostly at small farmers around his own political bailiwick in Lincolnshire.

Body's real achievement was to create genuine debate focused on the proposition that public support of agriculture always means money down the drain. He is for pulling the plugs on subsidies altogether, just as the New Zealanders did in 1986. This view induces something akin to cardiac arrest in the typical NFU audience and is openly derided by many fashionable commentators on the affairs of the industry. In Brussels, it is dismissed with haughty disregard. Even Mrs Thatcher's government, which has not shrunk from shutting coal mines, shipyards and steel mills rather than throw money at hopeless causes, remains seriously blinkered when thinking about what should be done about agricultural subsidy, though now willing at last to entertain drastic reforms to the structure.

Part of the reason for this lies in the consistent refusal of the Foreign Office to rock the boat in Brussels. Diplomats are afraid to take a robust line on the CAP for fear of calling Britain's European credentials into question yet again. This creates extraordinary exercises in double-think. When John MacGregor, financial secretary to the Treasury, addressed the rural worthies attending the Oxford Farming Conference in January 1987, he reported that farm support would cost the country £2,289 million in the next twelve months. 'By any standards, therefore, the Government's commitment to agriculture and the countryside is massive, has been increasing significantly and is on a scale not known to other industries.' Bearing in mind those last words, it is hardly surprising that the NFU's Simon Gourlay received a resounding flea in his ear from the Prime Minister for implying that farmers were being left destitute because of government policy. But the sensible Mr MacGregor then went on to attack what he described as the 'indefensible surplus race' between the EEC and its international rivals, fuelled by the 'misallocation of resources' which the CAP had imposed upon the European Community. MacGregor knows his brief only too well. Before doing these frightful sums at the Treasury, he manned the check-out till at the Ministry of Agriculture, where on arrival in 1983 he found a powerful hankering for the enduring melody of increased production at any cost. MacGregor edged remarkably close to the heretical Richard Body theme, invoking the general damage inflicted on the economy by devoting huge sums to the production of food destined only for the stockpile. But unfortunately, sound-money men from the British Treasury do not hold sway in Brussels. Control over agriculture is retained firmly by the farming ministers, and that means the sort of accountancy preferred by the Bavarian heavyweight, Herr Ignaz Kiechle, who denounced even the timid reforms trotted out before the European Parliament as irresponsible and impractical.

When the Germans talk like that, they generally mean it. Etched on every mind in Brussels is the memory of the 1985 price fixing, where a modest attempt to introduce some price restraint on cereals produced a German veto, the one-and-only occasion on which they have used it.

The bitter irony was that downstairs in another room, finance ministers from that same Bonn government were banging the table, demanding that the beast in the field should be fed no more money. Similar intellectual dislocations are common to the British attitude. Mr MacGregor's pious sermon to the Oxford host would cut no ice among a pack of CAP lobbyists in full cry. And British ministers, especially commuters from the Foreign Office, are only too willing to talk about the need to defend the 'integrity' of the CAP as an essential element of European unity – so long as they are preaching to the converted in Brussels – whilst swiftly changing tack to decry its follies when confronted by noisy backbench agitators in the Commons. This high-wire act is exceedingly difficult to perform with conviction, and when Michael Jopling fell off – or as some would argue, was pushed – during one maladroit performance in January 1987, the lack of any co-ordinated government strategy towards the CAP became obvious once again. The elevation of MacGregor to Michael Jopling's old job puts a red-blooded monetarist into the Ministry of Agriculture for the first time. Farmers reacted with predictable horror, but of course for them it is a frightful portent.

Of course Britain is isolated in her relatively bullish attitude in Brussels. Commission president Jacques Delors made that abundantly clear when he told Euro MPs that he was in Strasbourg to praise the CAP, not bury it. So the British government invests all its hopes in cutting and trimming the more obvious examples of waste. There appears to be no avenue of clear escape from the dense arboretum of agricultural subsidies, not even by restraint mechanisms which are equally costly to impose and enforce.

In the Beginning . . .

Sicco Mansholt, brooding at home among the polders, observes the carnival in Brussels with painful frustration. During the course of a long interview early in 1987, the old warrior toured again the fields of his triumph. Like so many veteran campaigners, he regards those who run Europe today, especially in the powerhouse, the Commission itself, as politically impotent. Why, in 1958, had not de Gaulle himself followed every detail of all Mansholt did with singular attention: the experts, scientists, statisticians, agronomists, trooped in and out, 'all contributing most positively to our deliberations'. The Commission eagerly beckoned into existence a pan-European confederation of farmers to help manage the emerging policy, the first example of the social doctrine of 'consultation' which would subsequently dominate all decision-making and frustrate reform. Mansholt positively sparkled as he summoned back these glorious memories.

But would he, with hindsight, arrange anything differently now? The answer was no. 'I would basically do the same – I would make no change to the system of protecting the market and no change to the common financing.' In other words, the agricultural featherbed provided by the irrevocable article 39 would remain entirely intact. Not even some form of price restraint, perhaps? 'That makes no sense politically – even a ten per cent reduction would lead to a great increase in people leaving the land, and many fewer farms.' And in any case, shop prices would only shrink by three per cent, far too insignificant to achieve any worthwhile increase in food consumption.

So where is the magic solution which has eluded all so far? 'That solution is to reduce the agricultural area.' The old Mansholt wizardry returned, undiminished. With powerful enthusiasm, he explained that by reducing the amount of land in production, the number of farms (and thus farmers) would remain the same. What he calls set-

47

aside would affect only marginal land. This would cut output to the order of 8% and swing the forces of supply and demand back into mutual harmony. 'Not producing is the only way to rid ourselves of the surpluses,' the Mansholt logic declares. Persuading farmers to leave part of their land fallow in return for a suitably attractive premium from Brussels represented the only escape route from the monstrous cycle of over-production, while at the same time preserving the farmer – his income, too – as the social guardian of the countryside. During this lengthy encounter, Mansholt dismissed in one sentence – 'I don't believe it' – the conclusions of a new study from Australia which suggests that lop-sided investment in the CAP, starving industry of the equivalent resources, has cost Europe a million jobs. And of a free market, where the entire baroque edifice of the CAP had been completely demolished? 'The countryside would be deserted. Of the five million farmers we have now, even a price reduction of 10% will leave just 81,000 with an industrial wage – and they will all be Dutch.'

Perhaps it is best to leave old men to their dreams. Mansholt acknowledged only one mistake in his original grand design. He and his collaborators failed to appreciate how the speed of technological development would over-take the industry. And on that he blames the surpluses – perhaps the only man in Europe to do so – rather than concede that the engine of super-production is also fuelled by prices which are set too high. He does agree now that even if his set-aside plan were adopted, then it might be put at risk by a projected 20% increase in food output in just ten years from the land still being tilled. Given the pace of development – and the nature of farmers – that looks like a glorious under-estimation. Any farmer who willingly agrees to surrender land will exploit what he has left with every resource he can throw at it – planting, as they say, to the white line in the middle of the road. The old structuralist which Mansholt remains cannot admit that less, not more, regulation is the only cure for the CAP. The all-weather canopy he erected over European agriculture in the early 1960s must be preserved intact. His is a voice which calls for the peasant and the yeoman to remain eternal keepers of that great contract with destiny, the European ideal. In this green and pleasant land, the new cultivators of the European economy – the soft-ware designers, the City yuppies so detested by M. Delors, pioneers edging ever forward to create new frontiers of technology, new generations born to computers and calculators – all are but distant figures in a vast landscape. It is an irrelevant, distracting vision, and one which has already cost Europe dear as she battles to maintain her position in the market places of the world.

As the interview concluded, Mansholt mused on what might happen to agriculture in tomorrow's world, and the prospects of reform. He values only giants from another age. 'There are no real statesmen now – the politicians are cowards. And there's no one left to take the long-term view, except perhaps for Mitterrand.'

3

A Chip off the Old Block

'Have a wash – in butter'

headline in the Star

The butter mountain is the most emotive of all the EEC's surpluses. Tory crusaders like Teddy Taylor have carved political careers from its alpine face. In Paris, a former shepherd, Jean-Baptiste Doumeng, who died in the spring of 1986, quarried a fortune by supplying the sweet yellow produce of Somerset vales and Norman pastures to Russian housewives at between seven and ten pence a pound. The price in a British supermarket wavers between 80 and 120 pence a pound. Yet despite even the most assiduous efforts of the man the French newspapers called the 'Red Baron', the mountain has continued to scrape the clouds over Europe, at the start of 1987 towering to 1,500,000 tonnes, equal in volume to the Great Pyramid. Less well known but equally problematical – one Commission official described it to me as the 'K2 of our mountain range' – is the associated stockpile of dried milk powder, containing in the first month of 1987 1,000,000 surplus tonnes.

The source of both is Europe's vast 26 million herd of cows, from whom the milk gurgles into the preparatory lake. Nourishing the dairy sector of the common agricultural policy costs the European Community about one-third of its entire budget, in the first instance, of course, in the form of guaranteed prices to producers. The gaping chasm between supply and demand then invokes another huge penalty: storage costs for manufactured products like butter and milk powder. In Britain the annual bill for cold storage is around £20 million and this has created a minor boom for companies maintaining the frozen stockpiles. They maintain a discreet silence when questioned by intrusive journalists about the morality of making profits in this way. So large had the bounty become by mid-1986 that the EEC considered colonising extra space in countries outside the Community.

As this reckless folly sweeps madly on, embattled officials are forced to admit that the only way to slam on the brakes would be to stop paying farmers nearly twice the world price to turn out the raw material for butter and milk products. And yet, they plead, those without sin should cast the first stone. This barb is directly aimed at the American government. The USA began the intensive subsidy of agriculture when fighting to support her collapsing rural economy during the depression of the 1930s. The cost has soared to $12 billion a year under the Reagan presidency, generating in its wake the depressingly familiar cycle of burgeoning output finding no genuine market. In the States, the major impact is in the highly sensitive 'corn belt'. That, as we shall later discover, is the fuse which lit the trans-Atlantic trade war between the Europeans and their American allies. Butter, though not a major weapon in the inventory, does however play a significant role, and Brussels will never lose the opportunity to remind critics of the CAP that the USA has around 73 thousand tonnes cocooned at preservative temperatures in subterranean silos.

Nevertheless, it is the EEC which remains the real sinner in the greasy world of international butter politics. As Peter Pooley starkly reminded me in his office in Brussels, 'The problem is now absolutely terrifying, not least because we are now actually holding 80 per cent of the entire world stock.' The French government, thoroughly obsessed with the notion of agriculture as the country's 'green oil' – it is no coincidence that 'Baron' Doumeng based his operation in Paris – castigates the Commission for its 'weak spirit', arguing that we only have so much butter because no one has been working hard enough to export it. This accusation raises a hollow laugh in Brussels, because there is in truth hardly anywhere on this planet, aside from the deficient markets of the Soviet empire, where butter can be unloaded in significant volume.

Dumping food on the Russians achieves no more than a temporary indentation, a 'chip off the old block' as Pooley cheerfully puts it. The wider consequences are more serious. Brian Gardener, who is the Brussels representative of Agra-Europe – an intelligence agency thriving on the business of reporting Europe's agricultural politics – has few doubts that the Russians cynically manipulate the CAP to their own intense advantage. 'We are playing Gorbachev's game. He is free to use his own resources to build up Soviet industry and technology, while dipping freely into our subsidy pockets to get essential food at cheap world prices. The Russians have an historic fear of food shortages, which might conceivably threaten the regime if they got out of hand. The conservatives – the forces ranged against Gorbachev – would seize the advantage from the radicals hungry for change if disturbances like those in Alta Altma recently became widespread. And of course, that cannot be allowed to happen.'

In Paris, Doumeng – now succeeded by a son of exactly the same name – ensured that the Kremlin demotes such fears firmly to the background. His sensitive antennae were always deployed to intercept the latest whispers that surplus food – grain, butter, milk powder, red wine – will shortly be put out for tender by the mandarins in the European Commission. The task is to strike for the best bargain, by exploiting to the full the cumbrous mechanism of 'stock disposal'. The Doumeng enterprise knows that Moscow will not buy at EEC price levels, which are inflated to around twice the average in the rest of the world. So there has to be a sweetener. This is where the bureaucrats invoke 'export restitution', a euphemism for another massive injection of subsidy – siphoned once again from the groaning taxpayers of Europe – to dilute those high-cost surpluses down to an acceptably biddable figure.

The arithmetic works like this. First of all the EEC pays farmers to produce food which no one realistically requires. The bill is sent to the 300 million people of the Community who are not farmers. They receive another one when the Commission is forced to store this unsaleable surplus. With figures now flying around the clock like digits on a Greek taxi meter, the search parties depart for likely customers to empty the cold stores and grain silos, before invoice number two (the one for storage) reaches impossible proportions. In the case of dairy products, the world is afflicted by glut, which the canny Doumeng exploited ruthlessly. The Red Baron's customers in the Kremlin insist on buying in at the lowest price they can get, playing the other major food producers, like the Americans, the Canadians and the New Zealanders, against the Europeans. What the Community describes as a 'tender procedure' is therefore a marvellous sham. World trade in food is conducted in dollars. If the dollar is weak, the export subsidy required to bring the EEC price down to the prevailing world price is small. A strong dollar pushes the subsidy into orbit. When a deal was clinched, Doumeng raked off a middle-man profit for himself and never denied that a substantial part of it was channelled into the coffers of the French Communist Party, thus helping to subsidise the Soviet propaganda campaign in the West. The Russians are thus the winners at every point.

Unusual secrecy – Brussels normally leaks like a colander – surrounds these transactions. The Commission maintains to the world that this is necessary to prevent price under-cutting by competitors. In reality, it is caught between the dilemma of exporting surpluses to politically unpopular destinations like Russia, Libya and Syria, which sour the image of Europe, and the desperate need to unload the food mountains at any price. M. Doumeng (and now his son) fulfilled a number of valuable functions, not the least of which is the opportunity for the Commission to conceal potentially embarrassing political improvidence by main-taining the pretence that they are selling to him and not to the Kremlin, still less to Colonel Gadaffi.

Of course any exporter of EEC surplus food may legit-imately benefit from subsidies. Doumeng simply proved cleverer than most in exploiting the potential to the full. His explanation was simple: 'I have the confidence of the men in the market, and I apply the methods of peasantry and Marxism to international commerce.' The old shepherd from Toulouse said this with a perfectly straight face. His company – InterAgra – is set for a profit of around $15 million on a turnover of $3 billion in 1987. Few visitors were ever deceived by his rubicond features, plump frame and studied air of detachment – just like a provincial inspector of taxes, one commentator observed. He always wore his communism lightly. 'It helps me with some, and irritates others,' was a typically casual remark. No one in Russia seems particularly irritated that most of the butter is shaved from the oldest portion of the EEC's butter mountain.

Andrew Pearce, Conservative Euro MP for Cheshire West, certainly did irritate the beadles in Brussels by revealing that the start of 1987 would see a massive disposal of 180,000 tonnes of butter behind the Iron Curtain, at the cost of £250 million in export subsidies. He described the venture as 'a gift to the enemy' and thought it better to dump the whole lot in the sea. Officials in the Commission considered his remarks malicious and spiteful, even though they had secretly studied the possibilities of chartering ships to dump particularly ancient butter into the deepest Atlantic entombed in concrete drums. Commissioner Andriessen gave the game away when he told informed questioners that rancid butter disposed of in that fashion might cause serious pollution. And in any case, as an anonymous spokesman declared, 'the option of destroying the stocks is merely uneconomic and defeatist'. Much better, he argued, to sell virtually a quarter of the butter mountain to the Russians all at one go. 'It is a fact that the Soviet Union is the only major potential purchaser.' Entirely absent from this calculation was the acceptance, tacit or otherwise, that as fast as the trains rumble eastwards, the cold stores are filling up again under the remorseless influence of the production carousel.

The interception of that carousel became the major objective of Community policy from 1982 onwards, when it became clear that the dairy sector alone possessed the resources to bankrupt the European Community. With ruin staring them in the face, the council of agricultural ministers at last confronted reality, or at least a degree of reality. They were corseted on one side by the treaty obligation to maintain the income of farmers, and on the other, by the immediate necessity to stop the flow of milk. On All Fool's Day 1984, the ministers suddenly banged down the sluice-gates. Milk quotas were born. The concept was not new. Sugar had been under quota for years, but compared to the dairy, sugar beet is a minor occupation for Europe's farmers, many of whom would now be restricted to artificial levels of production in a vital and politically sensitive sector. The buy-all guarantee remained in force, with the elegant additional mechanism that once farmers stepped over a certain level of output they would be penalised by a punitive tax.

The over-riding need was to get milk production down from a peak of 105 million gallons a year to something like 85. At that point, it was confidently predicted, the market would move into balance, the mountains would shrink, and the need to dump butter on the Russians evaporate along with the milk lake. Butter would not be cheaper in the shops, but no one in Brussels thought it necessary to mention that. Quotas were introduced during the French presidency of the community, an impressive display of political courage by the incumbent minister, Michel Rocard. In Britain, the NFU railed at the sell-out in Brussels. Their president, Richard Butler, declared that British farmers had been betrayed – a charge which bore little credence since talk of quotas had been grapevine currency in Brussels for months and his immediate predecessor, Henry Plumb (later ennobled as president of the European Parliament), sketched a theoretically feasible quota system in 1981. But farmers had been educated by their leaders to believe that the money-go-round would endure for ever.

In the event, the Rocard initiative proved a false dawn. Despite a modest strapping-down of output – coupled to a good deal of selective interpretation of the regulations in some countries – over-production returned to haunt the Community on an even larger scale by the middle of 1986. This time it was the turn of the British presidency of the EEC to turn the screws again. Farm ministers, led by Michael Jopling, struck out for Eldorado by aiming for a whacking cut in production of 9.5%. Flattered by reports of his epic, 28-hour negotiating marathon, Jopling left Brussels to the sound of champagne corks popping. The deal was scheduled to save £1,200 million in three years, but also bequeathed the carcasses of two and a half million cows which would now be inevitably slaughtered. In the short term this would add 600,000 tonnes of meat to the beef mountain, but everyone considered the price worth paying – a giant step, as Jopling put it, towards dragging the CAP back to the world of prudence and reality. Those qualities are invariably in short supply in Brussels, and so it proved within three months.

A Chip Off the Old Block

When ministers met again in the new year of 1987, they immediately launched into a fierce technical dispute as to what had really been agreed on 16 December. Headed as customarily by Germany, a long queue of recalcitrants – France, Belgium, Denmark, Ireland and even pocket-sized Luxembourg – queued up to register objections to the physical implementation of the measures by the administrators in the Commission. In the intervening weeks, the farm lobby had of course been working overtime, orchestrating a requiem of protest. In Britain the Milk Marketing Board roasted Jopling for delivering 'a devastating blow to the rural community'. They warned of creamery closures and massive job losses in the industries which feed off agriculture. And it was indeed perfectly true that cattle feed specialists and suppliers of milking equipment had responded to the first round of milk quotas by unloading jobs to defend shrinking profit margins. Politicians of all persuasions fretted over the inevitable economic consequences in fragile rural areas where employment alternatives are few. The same loud chorus was heard all over Europe. An independent commentator observed ironically: 'Market regulators are unpopular. They are costly, inefficient and often get power-drunk. Their strategies often lead to disaster and they will be blamed even for disasters they have not caused.'

The European Community chose quotas, coupled with financially-painful arm-twisting of their captive farmers, as a politically expedient exit route from one nightmare corner of the forest. In so doing they retreated, as always, from the real problem, that the CAP had wrecked the EEC budget and its agricultural economy, not to mention the hurricane trail of damage inflicted on the developing countries. These are the inevitable results of abandoning competition in favour of crude, short-term manipulation. The all-weather canopy erected by Sicco Mansholt turned out to be shot full of holes whilst the consumer was deprived of the protection of market forces.

The fate of the once-prosperous British butter industry is instructive in the folly of the CAP. For many decades it was the largest in Europe, the market consuming some 500,000 tons every year from all corners of the globe. Now that same industry is a miserable skeleton, with consumption still falling at the rate of some fifteen per cent a year. Within three years, experts are predicting it will shrink to the smallest in the 'yellow fats' sector in the UK. Bryan Hoadley, former butter marketing manager for the Danish Dairy Board, thinks that no amount of monkeying about with quotas or other artificial regulators can now make one jot of difference in the fight to survive. 'It is too late. The common agricultural policy has killed a market in which we were proud to work.' In a country where once butter was cheap, plentiful and commonplace on every kitchen table, it was demeaning to watch the senior citizens of Britain scramble for their so-called free hand-outs from Brussels in the winter months of 1987 – at a time when 46% of the country's natural production, some 90,000 tonnes, was being freighted to the nearest cold store. In a recent keynote speech, Michael Montague, chairman of the National Consumer Council, a government quango, lashed out at quotas as the source of high butter prices, which in turn set in train the downward spiral of consumption. 'It beggars belief that the Commission can be so out of touch as to fail to note the consumer resistance that already exists.' The chairman offered an olive branch to the farmers, whose logical coalition with consumers is another major victim of the CAP. His council opposed quotas because they forced the efficient and effective producer off the land. So far that call has received no echo from the dusty and ever-more remote chambers of the NFU on Hyde Park Corner, where in a fascinating sidelight on the 'Stockholm syndrome' – which psychologists deduced from the study of loyalty bonds established between captor and captive during a prolonged Swedish bank siege – Britain's major farming union has actually convinced itself that quotas, so long as they are not too severe, are good for the industry's health.

What a pity, then, that those who man what should be the consumers' advance post in Brussels still shy away from the energetic chaos of the free market. Tony Venables, the CAP expert in the Bureau of European Consumers (BEUC), drags out a wearying litany of more regulation when challenged to say what his organisation would create in place of the present riddled and enfeebled structure constructed from oddments of compromise and discredited economic theory. He endorses the Mansholt conception of paying farmers to take land out of production, favours handouts to persuade the elderly to leave the land, all of this coupled to 'more emphasis on environmental protection'. Perhaps it is long exposure to Brussels and its ways which makes him say: 'Whatever route to CAP reform is taken, compensation for small farmers will have to be taken into account.' Each one of these ideas represents an addition to the already tottering pile of regulatory controls. Certainly none of them will make even a minor incision in the food mountains, or brake what now seems to be the irreversible decline in the consumption of butter and other milk products. They are also guaranteed to accelerate the drift of the small farmer, the social guardian of the countryside, away from the land.

The EEC bureaucrats resist attracting blame for consumer dissatisfaction over the price and supply of dairy products in Britain by turning their fire on a major institution in the country itself. This is the Milk Marketing Board, a farmers' co-operative set up more than half a century ago endowed with virtually monopoly powers to buy every drop of milk in the land. The treaty contains a powerful inbuilt bias against monopolies of any kind (though some, like the airline cartel, for long bore a curiously charmed life). So it was natural that the role of the MMB became a major sticking point during Britain's EEC entry negotiations. In the crisp world of pure competition which the treaty prescribes, there was no room for powerful co-operatives backed up with monopoly purchasing powers. Having given away so much to the French already, the Heath government made a spirited defence of the milk board, and the result was a typical Brussels fudge. The board was allowed to continue its activities for a transitional period, at the end of which the dairy farmers – who are its sole shareholders – would be asked to vote on whether they wished it to continue. The result, very predictably, was akin to a general election in Rumania. It was also unique in the history of democracy, since cows – albeit by proxy – were allowed to vote. Farmers trooped along to the polling stations bearing a weighted vote influenced by the size of their herds. In the event, 99.5% of the farmers (the cows were less convinced at 97.3%) endorsed the continued monopoly of an institution which, in the countryside, has acquired a brand of sanctity associated with the established church.

This is because the board is the author of one of the most enduring features of agricultural life – the monthly milk cheque. Dairy farmers, the great majority of whom take no further interest in their product once the tanker trundles past the farm gate, regard 'the cheque' as the monthly chalice of survival. Many of them retain bitter inherited memories of the great depression of the 1930s, when their fathers were forced to peddle milk to dairy companies who ruthlessly exploited the weakness of a disorganised market. The creation of the Milk Marketing Board changed all that.

To the consumer, its most attractive feature has been the nationwide collection and distribution system, which for many years ensured a fresh pinta on every morning doorstep, thus fostering another folk institution which the British have come to identify with their national character, along with real ale and the monarchy. The threat to the 'doorstep pinta' was cunningly exploited by the milk board when the Commission at last acted to create a genuine community dairy market, which raised the spectre of bulk tankers rolling in from France aboard the Channel ferries, and thus a supposed threat to the whistling milkman and his clattering crates.

It was certainly true, however, that the creation of the board revolutionised the relationship between farmers and the major dairy companies, ending what the farmers were deeply convinced was a brutal system of economic blackmail. For the first time, they received a guaranteed price, no matter which dairy bought their milk. The inevitable result, of course, was that the price of the pinta rose inexorably – at an average of 23 pence it is now the most expensive in Europe and, some economists argue, the world.

The Eurocrats have also never forgiven the British for allowing the board to slip through a chink in the treaties. Ingenious minds are constantly at work in Brussels seeking ways to trim the power and influence of this anomalistic organisation. One opportunity gloriously presented itself when the board was directly challenged on the Byzantine hierarchy of prices charged to purchasing dairies for the milk it buys from farmers as the middleman: one for milk sold fresh and liquid, another for that later processed into butter, cheese and milk, yet another for skimmed milk, and so on. The so-called 'dual pricing arrangement' was indeed found contrary to the treaties late in 1986, although the board had already slashed through most of its pricing jungle in response to strong pressure from Whitehall. The timing of the verdict handed down by the Luxembourg judges was embarrassing politically. It came just as Mrs Thatcher was leaving for a major European summit and therefore tarnished Britain's *communautaire* credentials yet again. It was also costly, since the British government appeared obliged to repay some £5 million in credits received from the agricultural fund. And it focused the spotlight neatly on the centrality of the argument, namely the role of the doorstep pinta as a good deal for consumers when linked to monopoly control of the market. The *Financial Times* had few doubts. It warned: 'The present system, far from defending producer interests, operates as a substantial disincentive to consumption by keeping milk prices higher than they need to be. And without significant reform, the board's monopoly is likely to prove an increasing source of political and legal embarrassment.'

Naturally, the milk board does not see matters in quite that light at its beleaguered suburban headquarters in London. Nor does its handmaiden, the National Farmers Union. The milk board chairman, Sir Stephen Roberts, in the wake of the judgement at Luxembourg, had urged the Prime Minister to 'speak for Britain' in resisting further attacks from Brussels on his monopoly powers. But whose Britain could he mean? The virtually total monopoly the board enjoys by parliamentary statute ensures consumers are powerless to dictate prices, except by refusal to buy. And that is exactly how the nation's shoppers have been exercising their influence. The market for liquid milk continues to stagnate and the milk mandarins of the MMB, who should have been beavering away for decades making the 'marketing' part of their title mean something, proceeded to shoot themselves in the foot by producing a survey berating Britons for eating fewer dairy products than almost any other nation in Europe. We are almost bottom of the yoghurt league and tuck away only 7 kg of cheese per year compared to 21 kg in gourmet France. Luxembourgers swallowed three times our quantity of cream and, classically, according to the MMB 'we aren't even great butter eaters – 5.4 kg each, putting us seventh out of ten in the EEC.' And who, one may reasonably inquire, should carry the blame for that, if not the one organisation which has controlled the market for 50 years? The British topped the league on only one score – the amount of milk we drink. That is the one positive result, though an inverted one achieved by decades of obsession with liquid milk consumption – remember the 'drinka pinta milk a day' hoardings – and little else.

The board has also come under strong attack on another front. Not content with exercising draconian powers over milk purchasing, it has gone on to acquire a major segment of the processing industry through its wholly-owned 'Dairy Crest' subsidiary. This is mightily resented by its private-enterprise competitors who regard the board as an economic cuckoo occupying about one-third of the retail nest. Apart from surrendering its own statutory right to control the price of milk, the government has done precious little to trim the wings of the cuckoo. In 1933, the milk board was created 'by farmers for farmers' – there were no consumers to obfuscate the issue then – and ever since, the magnetic attraction of the postman calling with the milk cheque has exercised a myopic fascination for the producer. But the situation may be changing. More and more farmers, lured by the enticing pastures of the free market, are trying to break free from the MMB's suffocating embrace. The most enterprising are reinventing the doorstep round, injecting the added value of new milk products to attract jaded consumer palates. The Yorkshire dairyman who wrote to *Farming Weekly* early in 1987 was not the first to spot the glaring disadvantage of the Board's monopoly. He was receiving 76 pence a gallon for milk sold direct to the board. On the doorstep, that same milk has swollen in value to £2 a gallon. Squeezing into that profit gap is the motive for the expanding breed of independents – particularly in the new era of EEC production ceilings, because it can mean the difference between collapse and a viable future. However, these independent spirits are still forced to pay the obligatory levy to the milk board in order to satisfy its statutory right to buy. Many of them fiercely contest what they see as nothing more than a tax on

63

personal enterprise. Sparks may shortly fly. As the result of a vigorous campaign in a major dairy territory, Somerset, that purchasing monopoly may well be challenged by a group of renegade farmers. If the case does end up on the laps of the European judges, it might point to an historic judgement via the back door against an immunity preserved intact since 1933, and thereby bestow some unfamiliar smiles on the faces of the Eurocrats.

The custodians of the CAP have certainly had little excuse for humour in the past three years, as the insolvency of the Community moved ever closer under the pressure of bloated farm expenditure. The EEC is now so penurious that it lacks even the small change to attack a single major priority, that of melting the butter mountain. The so-called 'de-stocking programme' depends for its success on passing the hat around among the twelve member states – Britain's share will be about £400 million – with the IOUs being redeemed progressively as milk output falls under the new restrictions on output. As no one in Brussels bothers any longer to deny, the housewives of Moscow and Kiev will be prime beneficiaries of the deal. This is certain to provoke apoplexy in the Teddy Taylor regions of the Tory party. And as one folly succeeds another, thousands of tonnes of dried milk powder will be reconstituted as nutrient for young calves whose destiny it is to produce more of what we already have in excess. Necessity imposes no limits on ingenuity. The Commission is examining the metamorphosis of the more rancid quarters of the butter mountain into soap, drawing on the physical properties of natural oil. One British tabloid newspaper reported an official as saying that, if the soap option failed, 'We can always turn it into washing-up liquid – or burn it in power stations.' A longer stride from reality to burlesque is difficult to imagine.

4

Against the Grain

'And he commanded the stewards of his house,
saying, Fill the men's sacks with food, as much
as they can carry, and put every man's money
in his sack's mouth.'

Genesis, 44: 1

The towering pinnacles of butter are shame enough to the consumers of Europe. But compared to the granaries bulging with grain, they are small mockery. At the start of 1987, the Community had managed to accumulate 16,780,000 tonnes, which, if brought together in one place, would dwarf St Paul's Cathedral ten times over. The common agricultural policy has wrought a revolution in productivity from the wheat fields of Europe, and Britain – once a major importer of grain – has been transformed into not only a significant exporter but also the second largest contributor, after France, to the EEC's grain mountain. The attendant sweeping change in the pattern of trade has drained the west coast ports of the United Kingdom of their fruitful traffic from Canada and the USA. At Avonmouth, the sea-gate of Bristol, empty silos stand as monuments to a vanished age. The cattle feed mills which once thrived in their shadows have either closed or trimmed their operations to the minimum for economic survival, consigning hard-working and confused employees to the dole queue. But to the east of the M1 motorway, the East Anglian prairies – and that region as a whole – have witnessed a minor economic miracle thanks to the fertiliser applied so liberally by the CAP. Calculations have been made that if production continued unabated, then the unwanted surplus of cereals in Europe would treble inside five years. Britain's financial contribution towards maintaining a policy which offers guaranteed prices for every harvest, regardless of demand, exceeds by six times the amount invested in Fortress Falklands, and is half as much again as the government pays out in unemployment benefits.

Much of this is swallowed up by storage costs, which in turn – applied to all the surplus stocks of unsold food – consumes 50% of the entire CAP budget. The new agri-millionaires in Europe are those who built their fortunes on the profligate EEC farm policy simply by mopping up the overflow. One Scottish company made half a million pounds in a year by looking after barley nobody wanted. On just one small site near the Scottish borders, it was possible to find another 80,000 tonnes spilling out of four huge barns dominating a ten-acre site. The picture was mirrored throughout the country. In the five years from 1981 some 250 'intervention' stores, all but eight of them run by private owners, opened their doors for business. The storekeepers fought for anonymity, fearful of raiding posses of placard-waving protestors in the emotional tidewash which followed Bob Geldof's Band Aid campaign for starving Ethiopia. Civil servants do their best to extend the cloak of secrecy. But spotting the grain hoards soon became the contemporary badge of protest, often sported by those who were previously engaged in chasing cruise missiles. I was rung up in the middle of the night by a local news agency which had 'discovered' 50,000 tonnes of grain on a disused air force base in the West Country and bluntly interrogated as to what I intended 'to do about it'.

Stocks of grain on this scale are a wholly modern phenomenon in Britain. Responsibility for managing them lies with a special arm of the civil service called the

Intervention Board for Agricultural Produce, which is based in Reading. That is where the sums are done. It costs the Board about £12.50 a tonne per year to take in, store and then discharge grain – if a market can be found for it. The business of acquiring the storage space is sub-contracted to another quango, the Home Grown Cereals Authority. Accusations of excessive profit are naturally resented by those who stand sentinel. But in reality storage is an attractive way of generating profit at minimum cost. One major grain merchant told me quite freely: 'It's rubbish to say that there is no money in it. The quantities are large, payment swift and guaranteed, and of course the storage costs themselves, such as rent, are pretty low. And you don't need many people to mind the shop. It's a good living if you can get it – quite often for people who in normal circumstances would have little or nothing to do with agriculture.' Sir Richard Body was characteristically blunt. He called it money for old rope. The House of Commons public accounts committee came up with figures to show the true cost of maintaining cereals taken into intervention as £37 a tonne in 1986. And certainly the government did not trouble to deny that storage costs for grain alone had reached not far short of £190 million in a single year for an intervention stock of four million tonnes.

Expenditure on this scale forced Mrs Thatcher's government, dedicated to the tightest grip on the public purse, to perform unedifying political somersaults. In that respect, consider the sober figure of John MacGregor leaving his chambers at the Treasury to inform a rustic congregation at the Oxford farming conference that no administration in history has done so much to 'support' farming, whilst in the next breath flailing the reckless excesses of the CAP. The unpalatable truth is of course that any British government is powerless to rein in the galloping horses of the EEC's cereals policy by itself. That sealed contract made between the Founding Fathers and Europe's farmers at the birth of the community is the core of the problem. It has made the annual service of blessing at harvest home a mere formality, since every harvest is now a bumper one. That for 1986 weighed in at about 24 million metric tons, despite an indifferent climatic season, and not far short of the established record – 26.6 million tonnes in 1984. Rather less of that than usual was trucked off into old RAF hangars, but only because of the freak export opportunities following a prolonged drought in Spain and Portugal. That happy coincidence (for the EEC's pocket and the conscience of Britain's grain barons) is unlikely to repeat itself, because a potentially damaging trade war with the USA was averted only at the cost of re-admitting American farmers to the market they lost when those two countries joined the European Community.

The end result of the buy-all-you-grow system is that farmers bash the soil for all it is worth. One Norfolk farmer explained the mechanics. 'I use about three hundredweight of nitrogen per acre, which costs me about £5 a hundredweight. But that will hoist my grain yield up from two tonnes per acre to nearer three, and my turnover also rises, from £200 to £300.' With the safety net of high intervention prices waiting there to catch him should the natural price fall too low, our Norfolk farmer cannot lose, and nor will his French and German rivals when the combine harvesters move in.

The Norfolk example also tells us something about the way in which the CAP has utterly changed the economics of farming. Gone is the old pattern of a 'little bit of everything' – cows to milk, bullocks to fatten and a diversified range of crops to catch the market. East Anglia is now one vast range devoted to cereals, intensively pumped with pesticides and fertilisers to maximise output. The number of farmworkers in the region – they are rapidly becoming a threatened species – dropped by half between 1966 and the present day, the decline accelerating as the

CAP went into full swing. Huge landholdings which swallow traditional pasture and decimate copse and meadow, are now responsible for 15% of the nation's food output.

The consumer may be forgiven for struggling to discover some advantage in all this. None will be found. As record or near-record harvests become the norm, the price of bread continues to rise inexorably, once again inverting the laws of supply and demand. In 1986, the price went up by a penny a loaf. No one is interested in cutting prices, since all are trapped in the vicious circle of production chasing its own tail. The only smile is on the face of Jean-Baptiste Doumeng the Second, working out the calculations in his Paris office as the EEC's harvests are hauled from the fields. In 1986, his father obligingly bought 6.2 million tonnes of European grain on behalf of the Russians who will probably take another five million in 1987. In recent deals, the Doumeng team struck a price at around £60 a tonne, a shade over half the price that Brussels pays to put it into grain stores. That will translate itself into about sixteen pence for a loaf in a Russian bakery, that price having barely altered in the last twenty years. Food shortages are still common in the Soviet Union, but this is mostly due to erratic distribution and the fact that much of the home-grown crop either rots in the ground or disappears as the result of black market swapping between government agencies. But bread is plentiful, cheap and often given to cattle because it is much less expensive than feed grain. Ivan the Terrible would spin in his grave if he knew that peasants think nothing of throwing away stale bread – once a crime because the staff of life was such a precious commodity.

Doumeng knows that he can ruthlessly exploit savage rivalry between the Europeans and the Americans as they struggle on the world stage for the right to stuff food into Russian mouths, whilst at the same time arming themselves to the teeth to contain communism. This extraordinary spectacle is made possible by the fact that Europe's grain mountain is mirrored by a second, larger one grown in the USA. And the world itself is clogged with grain. The International Wheat Council predicts a global crop in 1987 at a record 1.36 billion tonnes. Even the Russians should manage about 210 million, which means the Soviet Union will be in the market for only about 23 million tonnes, her smallest international purchase for seven years. With total world exchange of grain likely to fall by 20% the prospects of the EEC chancing on some magic formulae to demolish the grain mountain once and for all in a totally stagnant market situation seems remote.

With the Russians as the only substantial buyers in town – and even then, eager to manipulate the best deal by forcing the EEC to compete with the Americans – it will clearly take years to whittle down the stockpiles. That offers no immediate salvation to the pressing problem of a Community budget which has long been outstripped by CAP expenditure. Nor does it ease the vast cost of storing unsold grain from one year to the next. And 'de-stocking' can only make a real dent in costs if something has been done to drastically curb the motorway effect of more grain pouring into the silos as fast as it is siphoned out.

The European Commission has tinkered at the fringes by setting higher quality standards on grain going into intervention. This marginal adjustment should discourage a few farmers from sowing in areas quite unsuitable for the crop, such as the land bordering the river Severn, until recently the preserve of sleek Friesian cows. One farmer here confessed to me, 'I could almost grow grain on a wet hankie in the kitchen, and they'd take it away.' Price restraint has also proved an ineffective weapon so far, because of fierce political resistance, especially from the Germans. Herr Kiechle in 1987 warned again that his government will resist 'to the ultimate' any attempt by the Commission to trim prices. In any case, agrarian surgeons know that, for maximum effect, price cuts must be draconian, at least to the order of 25 to 30%, a political price few of Europe's politicians would be prepared to pay. Quotas – like those introduced for milk and which have long controlled sugar beet production – are also regularly canvassed, but until now rejected by the Eurocrats because they cannot work out a way to police them. Only Britain, with its special quango, the Home Grown Cereals Authority, seems reasonably well placed to administer a practical quota regime.

Notwithstanding these difficulties, the SDP leader, Dr David Owen, trotted out what appeared to be his first thoughts on agriculture before a West Country farming audience. He seems, as farmers would say, 'to have stepped right in it', upsetting a strategic slice of the rural vote which the Alliance parties are courting. Owen clearly mistook his audience for a gathering of Washington eggheads who like to swop theories on zero options and medium-range missile gaps. For that, he suffered. He raced enthusiastically into a theme adapted from a double-tiered pricing system. This would automatically push grain-producers on to an escalator of descending prices when output passed a certain trigger point. The doctor's prescription did not go down at all well with his earthy, gumbooted potential patients. Simon Gourlay, wriggling on his seat with rage, interrupted the diagnosis to burst out that it would cause the death of the industry. Far from opening a peace conference, the SDP leader had walked unwittingly into an agricultural minefield wearing slippers. His two-tier system would certainly slash the profits of the 'big boys' in the grain business – the larger farmers who average 150 acres and more whilst leaving the smaller producers largely unscathed. 'Why should we be forced to subsidise small or inefficient farmers?' bawled one man growing 6,000 tonnes a year.

Hostility between large and small producers is indeed a new phenomenon throughout Europe, illuminating yet another glaring contradiction built into the CAP. In the

71

pastoral idyll conceived by Sicco Mansholt in the 1950s, the policy was supposed to underwrite family farmers who would in turn bolster the rural economy and generally potter about as social guardians of the countryside. But in fact, the real impact of the CAP has been to inspire massive farm mergers, particularly sprawling grain prairies. The small farmer will soon be an historical anecdote. Europe now extracts about 70% of its cereals from just 20% of its farmland.

Owen was on safer ground, though, when he exercised another fashionable theory, a tax on nitrogen, which attracts support because it seems to fire with two barrels at a single problem. Farmers, the argument goes, would spare the land if nitrogen was more expensive, thus cutting into the cycle of ever-higher output and, at the same time, mollifying experts who fear that nitrates threaten water supplies, especially in the intensive grain zones like East Anglia. The NFU sits on the fence on this one: a press release declared, 'We can't be held responsible . . . for farming practices over the past 30 or 40 years.' And of course, 'higher production from farm land was the goal sought by one and all.' Nevertheless, the union would co-operate with plans to cut nitrate levels so long as the EEC's proposals – 'arbitrarily low' – were resisted by the British government. The nitrate row is in fact a perfect illustration of the Alice in Wonderland character of the CAP. On one floor of the Commission headquarters in Brussels, zealots who want to clean up drinking water are furiously drawing up directives to control the use of nitrogen fertiliser, whilst downstairs a separate department is frantically writing out the cheques which stimulate farmers to use even more of the stuff. Somewhere in the middle you will find another group of distracted and disenchanted visionaries desperately wrestling with the entangled knots into which the CAP has tied itself, more or less in perfect isolation from their embattled colleagues elsewhere in the same building.

Increasingly, all roads appear to point to a single grand solution, and that is to take huge areas of farmland out of production altogether. This is what Dr Mansholt would like the Community to do, and tried to persuade it to do with his plan for CAP mark two back in the late 1970s. At that time, farmers reacted so angrily that on one well-remembered occasion a group of French farmers surged into the Council debating chamber with a rather confused cow in tow.

There is nothing fresh in the concept. What the Americans call 'set aside' has been a feature of their landscape since the early 1960s, when the USA's food mountains first began to look ridiculous. As a panacea, it has not proved a universal success. Bud Anderson, agricultural attaché at the American embassy in London, told a conference of cereal growers in Essex that set-aside was not the dream solution. It had partially worked in the States only because there were vast areas of low-quality, unproductive land to exploit in the wide open spaces of the Mid West. 'But that is not so in Britain, where much of the land is good, and should be switched to grow alternatives to cereals that are not in surplus.' The Americans are also disillusioned with set-aside because of its sheer costliness. In five years, the cost of the farm support programme in the USA has increased six-fold and it is time for the same painful decisions which confront the Europeans. President Reagan took time off from his 'Irangate' distractions to call for an end to farming subsidies worldwide by the year 2000. Much of that inflationary excess has been created by generous payments to farmers to grow nothing. In fact, the federal government has been cheated mercilessly. The sages sucking straw down on the prairies soon worked out that they could double their money by allowing their worst land to lie fallow – grasping a handsome golden handshake at the same time – while doubling their effort, and thus their money, on the land still in production. Democrats have denounced the administration's proposals – which include other radical measures like rolling cuts in direct incomes support by ten per cent every year – as a 'dead duck'. With the Democrats now in charge of Congress and a presidential election nosing over the horizon, that is probably beyond doubt in the short term. Just as in Europe, the farm-belt lobby is ready to throttle any significant cuts in government support. Bud Anderson says there are even people in the USA who would like to import the CAP, lock, stock and subsidy, from the EEC. 'Where it will all end is anyone's guess,' he told his audience wearily.

Enthusiasts for set-aside in Europe blind themselves to the reality that America's cereals output failed to shrink by any significant proportion under its influence. They also pointedly ignore the escalation it produced in the budget of the USA's version of the common agricultural policy. As usual, consumers have intercepted no benefit whatsoever. The only way to stop the dizzy madness of the CAP is to spend less money on it, not more, and given a chance, plenty of sensible Americans would say amen to that as well. Few of them, unfortunately, are farmers or politicians held in bondage by the farm vote. Good housekeeping – despite all the protestations in Brussels and Whitehall – is simply not in fashion when it comes to farm politics. When the British government began thinking seriously about the set-aside approach – in tandem with the brooding Dr Mansholt at home in Holland – Mrs Thatcher was reported as believing that only 'modest cuts were necessary to slay the monster that the CAP has become'. Prompted by advisers in the British farming Kremlin, the Ministry of Agriculture, she let it be known that cuts in cereal acreage of about five per cent would prove a happy medium – well short, however, of the swingeing 20% conceived by Mansholt as the basic minimum.

Brian Gardener, Agra-Europe's resident specialist in Brussels, was the first to point out the dangers of relying on back-of-an-envelope arithmetic. British farmers had expanded their wheat acreage by some 45% in ten years, turning the country into a major grain power for the first time. Nibbling at the fringes of that swollen prairie would make no appreciable difference to output, and thus the all-consuming cash appetite of the CAP. The modest calculations in Whitehall also ignored the technology by-pass. Productivity from arable land in Britain has shot up some 30% in thirty years, mainly due to advances in plant genetics, intensive development of pesticides and fertilisers and better mechanical equipment. It will not be too long before we see the first robot farmer prowling over the fields of Britain – indeed, the prototype already is. At the agriculture research centre deep in Bedfordshire, a giant mobile gantry is being designed which can perform every task from sowing the seed, to spraying and weedkilling, right through to harvesting the crop even in monsoon conditions. The mind boggles at the levels of increased productivity scientists and agri-technicians will contrive in the next 30 years – certainly sufficient, however, to make any exercise in set-aside intellectually redundant. As Professor Colin Spedding, presiding genius at Reading University's centre for agriculture studies, graphically puts it: 'It is more than possible that we shall conquer climate completely.'

But as the tempests rage around the future of Europe's food policy, the political climate defies rational attempts at control. When he announced the government's final conversion to the philosophy of 'soft agriculture' Michael Jopling expected to be illuminated by a shaft of sunlight through the gathering clouds: instead a violent new storm immediately broke right overhead. For a moment it looked as though Britain's farming (and, as he and his predecessors sometimes concede, food) minister had been struck by political lightning. What he did – only hours before addressing a hostile national gathering of the NFU, where an ambush had already been set in the form of a damaging motion of censure – was to announce a major relaxation on planning control in the countryside. The *Daily Telegraph* declared: 'The dig for victory era is over.' No longer would farmers be driven to squeeze the last ounce of food from every acre. Instead, the government would shift the emphasis to the 'environmental and economic implications of rural development'. Jopling walked into the Commons amid socialist jeers that he planned to carpet the land with concrete and conifers. To a man who had spent most of his adult life working in the countryside, these accusations were deeply wounding. The row opened up a serious breach with the Department of the Environment, which for months had been working on a new master plan for the countryside, temptingly code-named ALURE (alternative land uses for the rural economy). In the lobby corridors, Jopling was accused of poaching from a rival ministry in a bid to take the sting out of the forthcoming attack on him at the NFU. Ironically, almost everyone ignored the £25 million Jopling had scraped up to help farmers adjust to this brave new world. Those who did thought the sum derisory, which of course, compared to the vast bounty of EEC subsidies, it is. The row exposed to public gaze the long suspected fissure separating two major Whitehall ministries fighting for departmental control of what is increasingly called the rural economy. Mrs Thatcher reached for the political fire hydrant and expressed her full confidence in Jopling: too late, because what might have been a carefully controlled evacuation from the concept of total farming now looked like a rout. Jopling went quickly to the slaughter in the Prime Minister's post-election reshuffle. Absolutely no one was surprised except possibly Jopling himself. It is likely that no farmer will ever hold his job again.

British newspapers which reported the affair with such glee singularly failed to observe that the country cannot, by itself, declare UDI from the grip of the common agricultural policy: not, that is, without leaving the European Community altogether. The architects of ALURE have not yet solved that conundrum, either.

5

Until the Pips Squeak

Oranges and lemons, say the bells of St Clements,
You owe me five farthings, say the bells of St Martins.
When will you pay me, say the bells of Old Bailey?
When I grow rich, say the bells of Shoreditch.
When will that be, say the bells of Stepney?
I am sure I don't know, says the great bell at Bow.

traditional English nursery rhyme

Periodically, newspapers throughout the Community carry disturbing photographs of huge quantities of fruit and vegetables being bulldozed into the ground or fed to cattle. The resultant outrage is rhetorical, particularly when officials of the European Commission declare, hands on hearts, that the wilful destruction of perfectly edible fresh food is ordered in the paramount interest of the consumer. Yet very few people who witnessed the price of cauliflowers sky-rocket to a pound each early in January 1987, after Brussels ordered out the brassica extermination squads in response to an alarm call from the tightly-organised Dutch horticultural industry, considered it as anything but proof that the lunatics had finally taken over the asylum. Further evidence of that might have come from the revelation of the EEC's way of dealing with unwanted cauliflowers. They are soaked in cod-liver oil and then buried, the oil, according to official sources in Brussels, being necessary in order to stop people digging them up again. Within days, a sudden blanket of cold weather turned a glut into a shortage and the 'control mechanism' of the EEC's horticultural policy – the Brussels euphemism for creating artificial shortages in order to maintain the profits of growers – was once again centre of the political stage. This policy is a sub-division of the CAP and functions more or less exactly in line with the philosophy of rigid support for incomes, as the Treaty of Rome enjoins. It represents a complete inverse in one important respect, however. Instead of accumulating surpluses, the Commission simply commands their destruction. Still etched on many minds is the fate of Europe's bumper apple crop in the autumn of 1982. No less than 7% of a record harvest of 8.6 million tonnes ended up as pig swill or fertiliser, on the direct orders of Brussels. The apple-growers, fearing that a glut would send prices crashing through the floor, invoked their contract with the Commission to 'take out' the surplus. Europeans normally crunch through about 7 million tonnes of apples every year and so the bureaucrats maintained price (and profit) levels by eliminating the generous margin supplied by the rosy bounty of nature. The memory of what happened then still stings consumer watchdog organisations, who have persistently but un-successfully campaigned for the EEC to abandon a policy they have branded 'economically and morally unjusti-fiable'.

Of course, the odds are stacked against the consumer from the beginning. In most years, the Community is virtually 100% self-sufficient in vegetables, 83% in fresh fruit (that figure has risen since Spanish and Portuguese membership) and over 50% in citrus. As living standards rose, so did consumption, which spilled over into an expanding out-of-season demand for fruit and vegetables which Community growers could not always answer. Pitched against that are seasonal gluts, the limited shelf-life of the crops themselves and the fact that 'Community preference' – the system of me-first rather than an open door to cheap imports – distorts a competitive situation which would normally prevail. Perversely, that lock-out situation also applies to Spain and Portugal, who will not get tariff-free access to the full common market until almost the end of this century. This was at the insistence mainly of the French, who were determined to protect their horticultural industry from low-cost Iberian competition for as long as possible. Just in case the government in Paris wavered from that line, French growers stiffened its resolve with pyrotechnic displays of truck burning and cargo despoliation on the Spanish frontier.

The intervention system in the fruit and vegetable market was born in 1966. If prices fall below a level set by the EEC, producer organisations can get permission from Brussels to withdraw crops from the market. The aim is to stabilise producers' incomes by getting rid of excessive output which might otherwise threaten to depress prices. Eight kinds of fruit are thus controlled – apples, pears, peaches, mandarins, oranges, lemons, table grapes and apricots – and three varieties of vegetable: tomatoes, cauliflowers and aubergines (but not, as so many wits have observed, Brussels sprouts). The list has not been expanded since aubergines were recruited in 1982 and the one small victory consumer protests have achieved so far is to extract a promise from the Commission not to add any more.

Naturally, the entrails of the compensation system are exquisitely complicated. The EEC's upwardly-mobile budget meets the full cost, and the producer is 'paid' for the crop which will shortly be fed to pigs and cattle at between 25 and 50% of what the Commission reckons to be the normal market price. This may not seem excessive: but of course, the quantities offered for sale in the usual way – once the glut has been eliminated – are sold at an attractive premium. The producer, therefore, laughs all the way to the bank. Consumers simply have to swallow what they

can afford to buy which, as we observed in the contemporary case of the cauliflowers, will not be very much.

There is another classic irony in the intervention system.
The Commission is at least canny enough to work out that
unscrupulous producers could easily be tempted to dump
all their low-quality produce and then get a nice big
compensation cheque in the next post from Brussels. In
order to control fraud, therefore, the Commission is forced
to insist that only the biggest and best is fit to be destroyed.
It encounters real difficulty in making sure of that, because
thousands more bureaucrats would be required to scour
Europe on an endless Cook's tour, cluttered up with scales
and tape-measures to inspect each and every apple, pear
and aubergine offered up for sacrifice. The only solution so
far devised is a system of spot checks but, in fact, thousands
of tonnes of nourishing but sub-standard fruit and
vegetables disappear into the crusher. The EEC was
dramatically caught out in that style during the great apple
glut of 1982/83, and not long after a solemn edict came from
Brussels identifying new, larger dimensions for quality
apples.

Buried deep in the withdrawal regulations is a fig-leaf
which tries to mask the Commission's embarrassment
when ordering large-scale destruction. This allows fruit
and vegetables taken off the market to be given free to
'social institutions', such as schools, prisons and hospitals,
or handed out to the poor and unemployed. In practice,
this very rarely happens. And the reason is one sentence
which declares that food so distributed must be additional
to whatever quantities might have been purchased in the
usual way. As BEUC, the consumers' bureau, correctly
identifies, this ruling is open to 'controversial interpretation'. It is also pure camouflage. The Commission intends
merely to genuflect to social conscience because wholesale
giveaways would actually shrink the real market for
horticultural produce, a simple economic law which has

trapped the EEC elsewhere when it tries experiments like Christmas butter dumping. The net result is that less than 3% of the apples taken off the market in the thirteen years from 1970 were actually consumed by the socially deprived, the incarcerated or hungry schoolchildren. The remainder of the apple mountain was destroyed, fed to animals, distilled into alcohol or 'left to perish'. The illustration is even more graphic when put in sharper focus: in that same thirteen-year period, 1.2 million tonnes of perfectly edible apples were destroyed, eight times the amount – 150,000 tonnes – handed out as a gift of charity from the European Commission. BEUC has calculated that about two per cent of all fruit and vegetable output was officially taken off the market in the ten years to 1985, of which one-third was allowed to rot. The quantities withdrawn have also continued to rise inexorably, from 500 million to 1,278,000 tonnes. According to the Brussels-based Consumers in the European Community Group, in every minute of every day the EEC intervened to remove from the market 67 kilos of cauliflowers, 54 kilos of tomatoes and 1,100 kilos of apples. It should not be surprising that the cost of feeding this policy of destruction kept appropriate pace, rising practically five-fold up to 1984.

How can the bureaucrats justify these horrors? They are certainly bold enough to try. As critics multiplied, the Commission hit back with a special green paper, lashing out at 'misunderstandings and prejudice and over-dramatic presentation of the problem'. The document berated ill-informed comment for the 'negative reaction' which destruction of foodstocks invariably generates. No one, the desk-pilots moaned, had paused to consider the economic and social reasons for this type of intervention. Well, what are they? The green paper proceeded to haul out a series of self-justifying motives, most of which could be readily adapted to form quite acceptable articles of association for the Flat Earth Society. Deriving its text from our familiar friend, article 39 of the Treaty of Rome, the Commission's apologia rests on the need to maintain a minimum income for producers and 'a fair standard of living compared with farmers and people in other walks of life'. Few, I fancy, will consider aubergine planters and croppers of mandarins as among the more endangered species; and even if they all vanish tomorrow, no doubt other means would be devised to meet the pressing needs of society in those quarters. But lest we miss the point, the Commission grinds the issue down into fine, revealing detail. 'Fruit and vegetables always suffer from seasonal surpluses, which failing rapid sale can cause prices to collapse and expose growers to the risk of losing all their profits.' Consumers benefit because they are then guaranteed the best quality produce at reasonable prices. The indecorous role played by 'the relentless pressure of free market forces' is invoked only as a fearful warning.

Consumer organisations reject the withdrawal system as institutionalised robbery. BEUC points out that anything grown for humans and then fed to animals or left to rot in the fields can only represent an economic loss to society. The largest German consumer group points out that outside the special list of regulated products controlled by the EEC, it is quite usual for unsold, unwanted produce to end up being dumped by the people who grew it in the first place. No one compensates them, yet Europe has rarely gone without a lettuce for tea or a cucumber sandwich. As the sturdy Germans make clear: 'What is much more open to criticism is the EEC's system of legalising and organising destruction.' The Germans also have attempted to quantify the net advantage, if any, to the consumer. Their figures suggest that by interfering with market forces and the supply lines to shops and supermarkets, the consumer is charged about ten times what the EEC spends on 'support' (the polite euphemism for destruction) measures. As the innocent housewife sets forth to secure a salad for the family supper, she pays not only for the contents of her shopping basket, but for what has been thrown away as well.

Nutrionists have also fired their own volleys at the EEC's food destruction policy, which they consider a flat contradiction of sound-diet advice concerning the health risks of imbalanced meals. The young and elderly need fruit and vegetables for their organic acids and high vitamin content. The British Nutrition Foundation – whose director is the aptly-named Dr Richard Cottrell – agrees that as people are weaned off high-fat diets they need carbohydrates which come from starchy vegetables and the vitamins in fresh fruit. Those are precisely the commodities which the Commission spends a fortune throwing away. Nutritional quality is also completely ignored by the EEC's grading system, which is based entirely on size and potential eye appeal. This accelerates the trend towards monoculture, a dreadful bland sameness where variety used to flourish. As the German nutritionist Johannes Jaschik argues: 'The glasshouse tomato looks like a tomato but tastes of nearly nothing; the Golden Delicious apple is just a little acidiferous, tastes flat, but looks good.'

The wholesale waste of food is only one aspect of this conspiracy against the consumer. The EEC's legislators have thrown a protective net around the Community to control the access of imported crops whose offence might be to compete too freely. Here you will find cherries, plums, cucumbers, courgettes, endives, cabbage, lettuce and even artichokes. This list was further 'improved' by the addition of apricots and aubergines in 1984. It already included those other delicacies (minus cauliflowers) which are reserved for prestigious treatment under the withdrawal process. The European Commission fixes the market by setting the so-called 'reference' price, in other words, a barrier which imports must comply with before being waved across Community frontiers. Naturally, the reference prices operate at high seasons when EEC growers most want to dilute competition, or preferably, shut it out altogether. Invariably, that is what happens. This elaborate enterprise is another example of the EEC's pursuit of self-sufficiency at any cost. Once again, the consumer is deprived of access to huge quantities of cheap fruit and vegetables freely available on the world market. BEUC argues convincingly: 'It cannot be claimed that any of these products are of strategic importance. Choice and low prices are more important to consumers than a stable supply of each and every variety.'

The Community may pretend that it has the problem of fraud under control but statistics produced by the Commission strongly suggest otherwise. Watchdog organisations are convinced that the withdrawal safety net is now being openly exploited by those who grow excess crops simply to force the EEC to buy them up. In 1985, about ten per cent of all the apples in the Community came off the market, together with 7.5% of all Italian lemons, 27% of the Greek peach harvest, 2.5% of cauliflowers of every nationality and, just to complete the cocktail, practically 5% of all the mandarins grown in Italy. What the EEC has done is inadvertently to create a European horticultural industry based upon the principle of the instantly obsolescent apple. And, as we shall discover in a later chapter, the strange affair of the invisible tomato plays an important role in Europe's market garden.

Enlargement of the community to include Spain and Portugal, following the vanguard arrival of Greece in 1981, has given the EEC a distinct Mediterranean flavour – pear-shaped Europe, as some political geographers describe the result – and nearly all the crops the Commission fights to protect are Mediterranean in origin. There is considerable pressure, so far resisted, to extend the range, but compromise might indicate surrender in the face of the north-south divide which increasingly dictates political engineering in the Community. A major and possibly fatal step has already been taken in this direction through the 'Integrated Mediterranean Programmes' (IMP), a conduit created to channel resources and investment to the soft under-belly of the EEC. The Greeks have proved particularly adept in siphoning cash from Brussels to stiffen the rural economy. The Spanish and Portuguese, now they have lost the shine on their boots, are kicking hard for the same treatment. This means irrigation of dry soil, help to set up farming and horticultural co-operatives, aid for marketing and processing. It all adds up to greater output at more expense and irresistible pressure to exclude competitive imports from outside the Community. The Commission invests exaggerated hopes in production aids, so that more of the tomato and citrus crop, for example, goes to industrial processing – the canning factories. 'This should solve our tomato problem,' I was confidently informed by an administrator in the Palais d'Berlaymont who pushed a blueprint across his desk as though he had just designed the electric Concorde. He was dreaming of more pulped tomatoes squeezed into toothpaste tubes. This is a ragged philosophy. The Commission confesses in the latest digest of agricultural statistics that since population in the EEC remains practically static, consumers are resisting costly and artificial marketing strategies. 'Consumer behaviour' continues obstinate. The injunction to 'eat up your surplus' has not so far worked.

This is a timely moment to introduce Aunt Edna Pooley, an apocryphal lady whose nephew is the already-introduced deputy director-general of the agricultural directorate in Brussels. She streaked briefly like a meteorite across the warm Greek skies after remarks by Peter Pooley over the quality of the Greek raisin harvest. He told a British audience that his paternal aunt would not introduce them to her Christmas pudding – 'all straw and bits of stalk'.

Some weeks later Pooley received a clipping from a local newspaper in Crete, solemnly translated and despatched by the Athens office of the European Commission, strongly advising Aunt Edna not to look for a suntan in the Aegean, and certainly not in Crete, where the pride of the local raisin-growers was much injured.

Peter Pooley is attractively robust on the consequences of Greek influence on the CAP. 'It's like asking the mutineers to take over the ships,' he told me with disarming *glasnost*. 'They exploit the rules they like and then disobey the rest.' Now that the Greeks are in the EEC, raisins are the stuff of power politics. Like many others, Pooley thinks that the Turkish crop is better quality and certainly more suited to the requirements of the confectionery industry, a major customer. But the Turks are not in the EEC as paid-up members of the club (although they are burning midnight-oil in Ankara, sweating over the application forms) and under the association agreement, their raisin imports are bolted down by quota. And even if Turkish raisins are better, it is politic not to say so when Greek *'fonctionnaires'* are in the room – the 'Aunt Edna factor' as it is now known in Brussels.

Nevertheless, it took the Commission only a short time to appreciate the true cost of Greek entry when totting up the size of the Greek raisin and dried fig mountains. By 1983, when urgent action was clearly necessary, the EEC had found itself minding some 55,000 tonnes of dehydrated grapes and another 3,500 of mummified figs, all left over from the harvest two years before. A European Parliament report authorising the Commission quietly to dump the lot, patiently observed that the deteriorating quality of these morsels during such a prolonged period of detention made them difficult to sell – at any price. But the cost of storage to the EEC had already reached £600,000 per month.

It is small wonder that the consumers of the European Community have the strong impression that they are being squeezed until the pips squeak.

6

The Sweet Smell of Excess

'It would be hard to think up a more unjust,
wasteful and disruptive way of organising a
market for an agricultural product than the
European Community's regime for sugar.'

report from Consumers in the European Community

The story of what has happened to the British sugar
industry since Britain entered the EEC is a specific tragedy
for which the common agricultural policy must take all the
blame. The backwash has swept out to consume the
economies of small dependent territories in the Commonwealth, wrenching inside out the mechanics of cane sugar
production, a lifeforce of those mosquito-sized nations who
buzz incessantly at the ear of the EEC. A once-prosperous
refining industry in Britain itself has been brought to its
knees and may yet face complete eclipse. There is a
powerful argument that the EEC's interference in sugar
added another highly combustive element to the already
explosive international growth in the culture of illegal
drugs. All this has taken place against the background of a
slackening of the growth in world demand for sugar as a
basic product. In their latest sketch (1987) of agricultural
statistics, Commission artists painted a gloomy picture of a
landscape gummed up with sugar: 'During the 1980s, the
dominant feature of the world and community markets has
been over-supply. This has forced up stocks. These excessive stocks have depressed prices on the world market to

significantly below the level of the production costs in the world's most competitive areas of production.' There was more heavy weather to come. Excessive production would inevitably continue, whilst the development of artificial sweeteners, especially in America, could only depress the market even further. At the end of December 1986, sugar prices on *The Economist* commodity price index were bumping along the bottom at barely six cents a pound, which, as we shall see, means the sugar cane countries are scraping a living at subsistence level. In 1987 the world will churn out about 100 million metric tons, a modest rise in production but still another avalanche to add to those glistening slopes of sugar which already swamp the planet.

Orthodox medical opinion has been preaching for years that sugar is bad for us, the principal villain promoting tooth decay, diabetes and heart disease. One figure suggests that the National Health Service in Britain spends an extra £1 billion a year on teenage patients because their teeth are perforated with cavities inflicted by excessively-sweet diets, particularly fast foods like confectionery. But the evidence can be conflicting. A considerable rumpus has blown up in the nutritional world because a new report in 1987, from the British Nutrition Foundation, has torpedoed the established primacy that 'sugar is bad for you'. The health lobby is in a rage because the report undermines a positive link with heart disease and diabetes and suggests that the quantity and frequency of sugar eaten might be a more important factor than sugar itself. Say that at your peril in a world where the food we eat is highly combustible material for disputes among warring academics. Heavy counter-bombardment commenced almost immediately – 'whitewash', 'deliberate creation of chaos and confusion' and other such salvoes flew through the air. It seems hardly to matter. Complete eradication of sugar from the average diet is acutely unlikely but the fact remains that consumption levels will never recover to their post-war levels.

So the world is left with a good deal of sugar which no one really wants. And it is within that unhealthy economic climate that the EEC attempts to manipulate what it is pleased to call a sugar strategy and others describe as licensed asset-stripping against defenceless countries.

Like so much else in the CAP, what the EEC tries to do with sugar is essentially politically-motivated, and only distantly related to market theory. There are also two wildly opposed interests to reconcile: cane-sugar producers in the warm climate countries and the sugar-beet growers inside the Community itself. When the draughtsmen were bent over the blueprints of the Treaty of Rome, they naturally gave the beet producers priority, with barely a thought to external importers of sugar refined from cane. Only France, still clinging to the droplets of colonial empire scattered across the Pacific, had any significant obligation to sugar-cane; and that was eclipsed by the ambitions of the beet farmers – the highly protected *betteraviers* who dominate vast territories in northern France. In ten years, French sugar output has doubled and she is now the world's third largest sugar exporter. They find it hard to make sense of that in the Caribbean, where the plantations have been decimated.

When the British set off at last for Europe, they dragged in tow a series of large political steamer trunks, each containing a near-intractable problem inherited from empire. Chief among these was sugar. For the best part of two centuries, sugar and tea were vastly important commodities on the sea lanes to Britain. In the Caribbean especially, the great sugar plantations had dictated the complete pattern of economic development. The Caribbean economies survived and thrived on the sweet tooth of the British. The sugar they despatched across the Atlantic was cheap, went nicely with the tea and fed the most efficiently-organised confectionery industry in Europe. The quality and the supply never faltered. One company – Tate & Lyle

– became synonymous with sugar, owning and managing the plantations, refining the raw cane, transporting it home and then distributing through a nationwide network. Tate & Lyle made such a good job of this that the socialists could hardly wait to gobble them up. When the Attlee government set about nationalising everything in sight in the late 1940s, the sugar industry was high on the shopping list. 'Mr Cube' – the cartoon defender of free enterprise – is still a folk memory from the epic battles of that time. As it turned out, although doctrinaire socialism could be seen off fairly effectively, the real war of attrition lay ahead when Britain joined the EEC. Tate & Lyle traditionally faced insignificant competition from British sugar beet, at that time little more than a cottage industry hemmed into the fenlands of eastern England. But as the British prepared to transform themselves into Europeans, it was clear that a new breed of British *betteraviers* would acquire powerful support and a handy war chest, too.

From the moment that Britain joined the EEC, the Commonwealth Sugar Agreement (CSA) was doomed. This was an extraordinary institution, compounded from the spirit of post-colonial obligation and commonsense economics with a good dash of free enterprise thrown in to spice up the flavour. It represented the best deal the Caribbean producers particularly could expect to get. It is fair to say that not all of them were especially grateful. As many small outposts of empire took the high road to independence, they fancied that Tate & Lyle, and other companies like it, represented old colonial chains they dearly wished to shatter. The Caribbean brand of socialism, chiefly brewed by Manley in Jamaica and Cheddi Jagan in Guyana, ushered in an era of turmoil. The revolution turned sour as highly-efficient estates and plant deteriorated. In Jamaica, the economy almost collapsed and is only now on the faltering road to recovery; in Guyana (where Forbes Burnham expropriated Booker's sugar interests), it did. In Belize – formerly British Honduras – Tate & Lyle simply gave the land to the farmers, who proceeded to work it with commendable vigour. Yet always in the background the crucial Commonwealth sugar agreement remained a bulwark in difficult and troubled times, underwriting a specific passport to the vital British market.

An ingenious management system was devised to balance the interests of producers against refiners. This cocktail was made up of a good price to producers based on average costs, a healthy margin with efficiency incentives for the refiners, a guaranteed acreage and price for home-grown beet farmers, and another separate margin for British Sugar, the monopoly processor of beet. Like the giraffe, the result was clearly impossible, but it worked. The CSA shielded the Commonwealth whilst at the same time allowing competition – to the advantage of consumers – from the beet growers. When shown this eccentric constitution, the negotiators from the Six facing Britain at the entry negotiations declared that no amount of ingenious compromise could accommodate such a peculiar creature within the EEC's sugar regime. The British were told bluntly that beet came first. It was already clear that the key of the door to Europe would only be offered in exchange for a virtually complete surrender of Britain's old reliance on cheap imported food and a switch to the doctrine of Community preference. The Foreign Office, always a careless guardian of Commonwealth interests, wrote off sugar as an irritating and tiresome distraction which threatened to foul up entry negotiations. Had not, after all, our former dependents virtually spat in our faces by evicting trusted old retainers like Tate & Lyle? And to paraphrase Henry Ford, what did it matter where sugar came from, so long as it was white?

It became a question of clinging to some kind of guaranteed entry for cane sugar if Tate & Lyle was to survive at all inside the EEC. The cosy special relationship for refiners built into the old Commonwealth sugar agreement had gone forever, to be replaced by a new centre of gravity weighted heavily towards the support and maintenance of profit margins for European beet producers. Years before quotas arrived to menace the dairy industry, the Commission had peered into the future and found that it did not work. Production of sugar beet was soaring out of control. Rather than confront the beet producers head on and slash guaranteed prices – a recipe for political distress – the Commission selected the softer option of quotas. Theoretically, each country would henceforth unselfishly agree to a share of the cake, linking production to consumption. But the uproar followed just the same. After a series of ferocious disputes, the usual faint-hearted compromise appeared and sugar production ran out of control regardless. We now grow four million tonnes above our basic sugar beet requirement in the EEC, 70% above the Community's most generous requirements. This is the source of a massive cavity in the EEC budget.

Heads were now aching at Tate & Lyle. Britain's entry deal set up a 'cane quota' for the EEC, 90% of which would continue to be shipped to Britain for refining. This spineless compromise ensured from the start that there could be no cane mutiny, since the refiner – in essence, Tate & Lyle alone – had no leverage over the political machinery in Brussels. Even when the EEC set up its own pact with the developing world in 1975 – 66 countries have now signed the Lomé Convention, mostly former British and French colonial territories – the Commission continued its cavalier attitude towards the cane industry, dismissing it as a 'British problem'.

Understandably, the cane-producing countries have a different view. They resent the paternal grip the EEC maintains over them. This is mostly exercised through the 'sugar protocol' system. A quota of cane sugar is allowed into the EEC (in practice, only Britain), and the producing countries get the guaranteed price paid for beet sugar inside the Common Market. This is not the happy arrangement which at first it seems. Because the EEC is such a monolith in the world sugar business and produces a beet sugar mountain, the Lomé countries find it difficult to sell elsewhere on the world market. They consider the price they get through the protocol – worked out in the EEC's mythical ECUS – excessively mean, despite an additional topping-up of £85 a tonne by Brussels. In Euro currency terms, the EEC's price for cane sugar has not increased for nearly five years. So many developing countries who are squeezed to find an alternative source of income end up selling sugar to the EEC for not much more than it cost them to produce it, although some well-organised countries like Malawi and Swaziland do reasonably well.

Tate & Lyle had lost an empire and failed to find a new role, for which they are still desperately searching the best part of twenty years later. They found themselves frozen on a refining plateau of about 1.1 million metric tons a year. Away in the fens, however, thanks to the new fertility bestowed by Brussels, sugar beet production had broken free of the shackles of the Commonwealth sugar agreement and soared skywards to meet its quota of 1.144 million tonnes (although the British *betteraviers* still scream for more, because they consider their beet quota inadequate). Under the old system cane and beet could never reach equal footing. Now they have, Tate & Lyle is compelled to compete with British-grown sugar at prices which are rigged in favour of beet. Gone are those heady pre-EEC days when Mr Cube's refineries churned out annual profits in excess of £4 million. At the company's riverbank headquarters at Sugar Quay in London, they still speak with misty eyes of the 'genuine partnership' between producer and refiner which existed in the old days: under the sugar protocol which now prevails, all the refiners are excluded from price negotiations. This matters not a jot to the beet refiners, who are doing very nicely in a climate effectively run by and for the benefit of the growers of their basic raw material.

The result is a sticky, congealed mess, 'like walking through molasses wearing paper shoes', in the words of one harassed Commission official. And as Kenneth Fleet clinically observed in his *Times* column, 'the system is fundamentally unsound.' This became desperately obvious when Europe resounded to a bitterly-fought take-over battle in the sugar industry. In 1986, Tate & Lyle set out belatedly to re-conquer the empire it lost when Britain entered the EEC. The company tried to swallow the British sugar beet industry at one go by making a bid for British Sugar. Unfortunately, an Italian rival was already wooing. And for a while, a third suitor hovered uncertainly on the fringes. At the end of 1986, however, it looked like a straight fight between a re-invigorated Mr Cube, freshly horsed on a new charger, and the Ferruzzi group from Italy (who number among their cavalieri none other than Sir Richard Butler, formerly in command at the NFU). The National Farmers Union managed to wrong-foot itself almost immediately, pleading for the special status of British Sugar as a 'strategic national asset.' In a world choking on sugar the argument appeared more than usually weak. But it dovetails perfectly with the union's dislike of imports of any kind, especially from competitive Commonwealth producers. As it happened, the nuptials were frustrated by the Monopolies and Mergers Commission, whose recommendation that both the Tate & Lyle and a separate Italian bid be blocked was subsequently confirmed by the Industry Minister, Paul Channon. There was much tea and sympathy for Tate & Lyle, who had no further opportunity to secure their position in the UK market. This may mean, as the company has warned, the closure of their cane refineries in Greenock and East London (the Liverpool plant and three others have already been axed). And if that happens, the cane-producing countries will lose their toe-hold in the EEC and the entire, cumbrous sugar protocol will collapse in ruins. The further turmoil this will induce in fragile Caribbean economies is not a happy prospect.

Passing down its judgement, the Monopolies Commission directed another salvo at Brussels, describing the European sugar industry as afflicted with an 'accumulation of guarantees, controls and quotas'. This soothed few bruises down at Sugar Quay. Nor did the suggestion that the British Government should knock sense into its Community partners' heads by getting them to agree to fairer profit margins for the EEC's only significant cane refiner. The other alternative rehearsed was a direct subsidy to Tate & Lyle, a proposition certain to lodge in the throat of a free-market government. The City concluded that the affair measured once again the lunacy of the common agricultural policy. The sugar row also coincided with public concern over the Guinness affair and lurid opposition attacks on merger policy. This certainly influenced Paul Channon's swift decision to squash both the British and Italian bids. The minister was badly advised because the future of British Sugar as a company has nothing to do with free enterprise, and should Tate & Lyle abandon cane producers to an unnatural fate, then British Sugar will inherit an automatic monopoly without another shot being fired. The Monopolies and Mergers Commission similarly misread the situation, and clearly failed to swot up the history books on the miserable story of sugar since Britain went into the EEC. Of course the situation would be transformed if Brussels could be persuaded to introduce some elasticity into the cane-refining margins. Hymns of joy would be sung all over the Caribbean (and in Mauritius and Fiji too) with cheerful refrains from London's Sugar Quay. Their song would be drowned, however, by the chorus of protest from the European sugar

95

beet industry. The prospect of the French in particular surrendering their primacy appears infinitely remote.

The 'frigid bureaucrats in Brussels' – as a Gaullist Euro MP once described them – also appear indifferent to what is happening in the sunny tropical islands where cane is grown. The economy of Jamaica, which has witnessed so much turmoil in the sugar industry and the virtual collapse of another staple export-earner, bauxite, now faces the grim prospect that its future may be ransomed to marijuana. For many years, it has been the basis of the island's underground economy, with heavy trafficking to the United States. In the league of suppliers to American smokers, narcotics control agents now reckon that Jamaica is in fourth place. Everyone who visits Jamaica knows how deeply 'ganja culture' – openly proclaimed by the Rastafarian cult – has eroded the island's social and economic foundations. Despite all the denials from Edward Seaga's proud reforming government, the creation of the 'double dollar' – one official, for internal circulation, and the other rigged at a special rate for visitors – amounts to the tacit recognition of ganja as a means of exchange. Illegal exports of marijuana are reckoned to be worth $500 million a year. The country's national airline has even been threatened with losing its permit to land in the USA because drugs have been so frequently discovered among cargo. Official crackdowns, including helicopter swoops on ganja plantations, have failed even to dent the trade. And the destruction of marijuana crops merely exposes the fragility of the Jamaican economy. In the Westmoreland parish in the west of the island, a local pastor explained the situation bluntly: 'What we are seeing is the devastation of entire villages which had been built on cultivation and sale of the drug. How do we get these people to go back to planting potatoes?'

Or, for that matter, sugar. With its price now scraping the bottom of the barrel at six cents a pound – and no room to expand exports of other tropical crops like bananas – Jamaica is trapped in a straitjacket imposed on her by external trading partners like the EEC. During pre-nationalisation days, Jamaican production was in excess of 400,000 tonnes, and the figure has now slipped to less than half of that. At this level, Jamaica has insufficient sugar for home use and the EEC and American quotas – so to meet all those demands, she actually imports from the world market, which is like selling sand to the Saudis. Some 20,000 sugar jobs have already vanished in Jamaica, too many for a small island community aching with unemployment and poverty. One obvious answer would be to cut back on European beet sugar production, so that cane could win a bigger share of the still-huge EEC market. If the Community had such courage – and faced out the inevitable backlash from the beet growers and their political friends – then it would be possible to stiffen the backbone of threatened sunshine economies. The Lomé Convention would look more like a pact of friendship than a lop-sided cartel.

Many administrators in Brussels freely advocate trade rather than aid as the keynote of the EEC's development policy. They are mostly ignored. Despite copious bouts of hand-wringing about the fate of developing countries lashed to the rack of static economic development, such radical thinking has made no progress against the entrenched philosophy of agricultural isolationism, the hallmark of the CAP from its inception.

Each winter, the mighty beet harvest is hauled from the fields of Europe. The long roads of northern France and the English fens are choked with tractors grinding slowly to the sugar mills. By the spring, this always means a gigantic accumulation of sugar stocks. In March 1987, the total weighed in at 11,170,000 tonnes. This shifting dune will shrink as the year wears on: but the size of the bitter-sweet problem Europe refuses to confront remains exactly the same.

7

A Butter Cream Tart
and the Pork Carousel

'Although one fraud may be more complicated or
cunning than another, they all follow the same
basic pattern.'

Green Europe, EEC newsletter on the CAP

Just how much money flows down the drain because of
frauds committed against the common agricultural policy
has never been fully established. Bob Battersby, Tory Euro
MP for Humberside and himself a former EEC official,
believes it might be '£30 or £40 million'. The House of
Commons select committee on agriculture considered that
between 1976 and 1978, about £11 million was siphoned
away by imaginative exploitation of the CAP. Brian
Gardener of Agra-Europe suggests that a more realistic
figure would be around twenty per cent of the entire bill for
the CAP, which suggests deception on a titanic scale since
the farm policy was scheduled to cost the Community £17
billion in 1987. The budget control committee of the
European Parliament has wearily concluded that 'virtually
no form of Community finance is untouched by frauds and
irregularities in almost every sector', whilst Professor Klaus
Tiedemann of Freiburg University, a specialist student on
'economic crime', dismisses the CAP as one of the most
lucrative fiddles in the whole of Europe.

The European Commission are acutely sensitive to the
suggestion that they have left the tap running and lost the

telephone number of the plumber. It must be someone else's fault. By 1980, when a number of well-publicised cases suggested that exposed fraud represented the tip of a submerged iceberg, the Commission began to file their defence with a secret internal dossier. Early in 1981, this was obligingly leaked to *European Report*, a news-sheet whose avid readership is composed entirely of informed Berlaymont-watchers. The exposure shamed the Commission into open publication a year later. 'Safety first' seemed to be the motive. Whilst Community regulations were complex, attempts to simplify and clarify the rules were impeded by 'the ever more complex mechanisms of international business, mechanisms adopted by the traders themselves'. Orwell's 1984 had arrived, two years ahead of itself. So far as the Commission were concerned, the plumbers themselves were responsible for all the broken pipes through which the taxpayers' money gushed.

The Commission's case never looked as though it would hold water. One massive source of leakage is the complex network of border control taxes for agricultural products known as MCAs (monetary compensation amounts) which provide a remarkable opportunity for profit. The great Italian butter-go-round stands as a perfect example. This massive swindle alone cost the European Community nearly £5 million. It was organised with the clockwork precision of a well-planned military operation. A ten-man team, working through three companies, established control headquarters in Switzerland, the non-EEC island stationed at the crossroads of Europe. The plausible basis was the export of 6,000 tonnes of surplus butter from Holland to Italy. An armada of no less than 248 lorries was assembled and as each one lumbered over the Italian frontier, the precious cargo aboard automatically collected a special export subsidy – using forged documents, as it later transpired – direct from the coffers of the EEC. But the butter never reached the east. It would be pleasing to record that eagle-eyed investigators from the EEC had unmasked the plot by planting themselves in the butter fleet in disguise. But sadly, this brilliantly-devised sting fell to pieces when one lorry broke down and awkward questions were asked about the destination of the butter stacked at the back. It is hard to square this single incident with the Commission's insistence that 'traders themselves' have complicated the system beyond endurance, since border control taxes on food and export subsidies are entirely the genius of the European Community.

Butter has always proved an irresistible attraction to crooks, because the EEC has so much of it and the ramshackle apparatus of the CAP creates endless loopholes for the unscrupulous. Perhaps nowhere else in the civilised world do squads of customs officers suddenly pounce on supermarkets and seize butter as though it were pirate gold. Yet that is precisely what happened in Belfast in 1980, when suspicion was aroused by bargain offers tempting housewives at 20p per pound below the usual EEC price. A loss-leader perhaps, or something more sinister? What the authorities uncovered was a lucrative fiddle made possible by artificial distortions under the CAP and the rambling, unsupervised border between Ulster and the Irish Republic, which we shall further explore later. Butter produced in the South had received lavish EEC and government subsidies to the tune of around £400 a tonne, £200 of which should have been repaid for every tonne sent out of the country. Instead, huge quantities were smuggled at night over the border into the north, there to be sold at an attractive premium. There were claims at the time that the IRA was exploiting the largesse of the CAP as a fund-raising exercise.

The affair of the butter cream tart concerned another ingenious stratagem to avoid paying the full price for butter. Community regulations declare that old stocks no longer fit for direct consumption can be sold off to bakers and confectioners at much reduced prices. The Commission's own report explains how one firm ended up being hauled into court for baking fancy cakes that broke the rules. Instead of using the butter to make pastry, it prepared a sort of sandwich biscuit which consisted of thick slices of butter placed between thin layers of biscuit. At a later stage, it was then extremely easy to remove the butter for other purposes. In the trial which ensued, the firm in question tried to convince the court that their product was a 'butter cream tart' which it would be perfectly correct to describe as a pastry product. If the Founding Fathers of the European Community were now suddenly resurrected, it is hard to say what they might make of their offspring prying into tarts, with the full majesty of the law to back them up, while the plundering Japanese pound at the gates loaded with computers and video-tape recorders the Europeans do not make.

Since the Irish Republic's government hurried the punt into the European monetary system, breaking the long-established customs union with the UK, the border between north and south has turned into a playground for CAP fraudsters. To unravel the case of what is now enshrined in Community mythology as the 'Castleblayney Trail', we must descend into pure farce. Our hero is an unnamed customs official, sentenced to the well of loneliness at the Carrickcarnan border post between Dundalk and Newry. The local geography is complicated by a sliver of Ulster which juts into the south, bisected by a narrow border road christened the Castleblayney trail after the principal local village. Such a station in life gives one plenty of time to think, in this case on the rhythm of a particular lorry which appeared at the border post at the same time every day, loaded with barley and all the paperwork to claim an instant export subsidy. Why, the border sentinel puzzled, did the lorry always arrive so late in the afternoon, given that considerable time was clearly required to reach its destination in the north, unload the barley and then repair back to the Republic before nightfall? After this routine had repeated itself for some days, the sleuth decided to trail the lorry, 'green book' in hand to record the facts. Once again the truck arrived, cleared its 525 sacks of barley, clicked up the export refund and rumbled off in the general direction of Belfast. Unknown to the driver, he was not only being tailed but also watched through binoculars from a second post which commanded a perfect view of the salient of Ulster territory through which he now trundled. His ruse was magnificent: he had collected a handsome purse at one border crossing, but he now intended to head straight for another and go for the double. He had also discovered the secret of how to transform base materials into gold, for a hundred of the sacks contained seven tons of sand. How much money the EEC had lost in this cycle of perpetual motion has never been discovered. Not the least fascinating detail was a map of the encounter, resembling a clipped-off fragment from the Battle of the Bulge.

It is in these border regions of Ireland that agile pigs might fly. It is beyond question that a large number have become exceptionally dizzy, perhaps even travel-sick. For a while the pork carousel, as it became known in Brussels, was an enduring feature of the straggling border between the two Irish communities. The origins of the carousel lay in distorted subsidies. At a time when the UK enjoyed a 30% advantage on farm goods imported from other Community countries, astute livestock breeders in northern Ireland swiftly calculated the gains to be made from additional mobility in their herds of swine. By walking them over the border under the cover of darkness, they could be re-introduced to their old home the following morning, generating a net profit of some 27% – the Republic suffering from only a modest advantage of 3% under the subsidy umbrella. When, like the earth's magnetic field, the subsidies periodically reversed themselves, so did the carousel. The practice became quite sophisticated. One regular pork-runner excavated a tunnel for the convenience of himself and his migratory beasts. Others abandoned the tiresome business of keeping pigs altogether and simply hired them for these profitable peregrinations. This enterprising industry was stalled when the pigs were issued with passports – dead or alive – in the form of indelible marks declaring their origin. The Commission wrote this happy sequel – 'And so the merry-go-round was brought to an end.' But can we be sure? A spot of ink on a pork carcass will rarely deter an imaginative entrepreneur.

And certainly not, it would appear, on the leaky frontier between Belgium and France, which sheep may safely cross once equipped with Belgian slaughterhouse stamps and certificates or origin from the Belgian authorities. The French are historically resentful of British lamb imports, whilst incapable of meeting demand on their own market. This breeds a powerful sense of frustration among both parties. In the early 1980s, 6,000 to 7,000 tonnes of English lamb, posturing as pure bred in Belgium, arrived for sale at the great Rungis wholesale meat market south of Paris. The Germans and the Dutch took a hand in an evidently lucrative trade, imaginatively designed to overcome steep import levies. The 'lamb war' between the British and the French eventually assumed such proportions that an entirely new regime was created to introduce a sense of order. Since then the Belgian border has been quieter, but occasional skirmishes continue whenever the French feel that perfidious Albion is breaking the rules. The strange cosmic forces which rule the EEC have also ensured that a quite different set of rules continue to govern the trade in meat: industrial manufacturers inside the Community have recently been forbidden by edict from Brussels to stamp their goods with the country of origin, yet to prevent wholesale fraud in the agricultural sector, there is a licensed system of carcass marking.

The Commission's bulging dossier documented one example of how meat may not always be quite what it seems. The file was labelled, with splendid under-statement, 'mortadella of a doubtful composition'. The villain of this piece was an Italian sausage manufacturer who imported 45 tonnes of pork with the declared intention of making mortadella for subsequent resale outside the Community, an arrangement which stood to win him 350 million Italian lira (approximately £168,000) through perfectly legal exploitation of customs levies. But the pork never left Italy again: it was sold on the local market at an attractive profit. To comply with the conditions of sale, the sausage-maker let his culinary imagination run riot. He manufactured a strange 'mortadella' from a mixture of horse-dung, sawdust and cotton, which he then 'sold' to imaginary firms in Greece and Spain (both at that time outside the EEC). The fraud was detected by an unusually valiant customs officer in Genoa who opened up the consignment and tasted it. Sadly, the record is silent on his reaction. The sausage-maker went to prison for four years.

Wine is another dubious commodity. The European Parliament believes that the Community has been robbed of tens of millions in every year since 1976 through elaborate manipulation of quantities of wine sent for industrial distillation. Figures so far produced are described as a 'conservative estimate'. And the budget control committee are convinced that the true figures are being hidden.

Tax-payers' money has also been frequently employed to circulate large quantities of waste – boxes of bones and old meat unfit for consumption – around the Community. As always, the trick is to intercept border subsidies. A classic example was the German dealer who hit on the idea of packing export containers with rubbish while declaring the consignment as top-quality beef. An importer in the United Kingdom played the role of fake recipient for a share of the proceeds. The waste left Germany deep-frozen in polythene bags, concealed beneath a few packs of genuine beef. Each container was accompanied by an impressive forgery of the appropriate German slaughterhouse stamp, perfectly finished down to the last Teutonic detail with a customs seal created from the imprint of a one-mark coin. This time there had been a tip-off to the British customs. The Commission was able to rejoice – 'the culprits were severely punished.' Yet it is an open secret on the Brussels grapevine that the flourishing underground trade in fake meat continues almost unhindered. The budget control committee of the European Parliament is constantly presented with evidence of fresh irregularities at the frontiers. The rich pickings to be made from exploiting the EEC's complex net of border taxes and subsidies are irresistible. Entire phantom cargoes swish undetected under the noses of customs officers every day. The frauds are increasingly subtle and now encompass almost everything on the menu of the CAP: Iranian caviar smuggled into Denmark, declared as water melons; a ten-year racket on the German border linked to forged certificates for Austrian cattle; a Danish variation on that old stand-by, the merry-go-round, this time with cheese instead of butter; the bizarre affair of Jamaican sugar transformed into 'artificial honey' in a free zone; fish offered for intervention when it had already been sold; raw coffee supposedly bound for eastern Europe sold instead to manufacturers in Germany; Greek oranges multiplying like the loaves and fishes when offered for the infamous withdrawal procedure – the list goes on and on.

Italy in particular has long proved a happy hunting ground for inspired swindling. This is partly because all Italians display a healthy disrespect for ordinance of any kind, and national laws, let alone EEC regulations, are often enforced but fitfully. But there is another, more sinister factor, the long reach of the Mafia, for whom the multitudinous complexities of the CAP exercise a compelling attraction. Italy's main contribution to the common market in food is olive oil, an industry which provides a livelihood for about a million families, many of them in the poor south and Sicily. Figures suggest a total of about 200 million olive trees in Italy, but no one really knows for sure since, as Bob Battersby has cogently pointed out, the system of counting them has hardly changed since the days of the Romans. The oil is milled in some 8,000 refineries, many of them shack-and-chimney affairs tucked away in the hills. Keeping track on how much oil is refined each year, and then matching the result to claims made against the CAP, would require an army of 50,000 controllers, about six times the entire current administrative personnel of the EEC. No wonder Brian Hord, former Euro MP for London West, was moved to describe the olive oil regime as a gaping black hole into which money poured, never to reappear again.

As Hord told the European Parliament in 1984: 'We do not know how many olive trees there are, though counting started back in 1978. We do not know how much olive oil is produced. And we do not even know how much is consumed, or by whom'. What did become clear, however, was systematic embezzlement creaming some £80 million a year from ghostly groves of olive trees, with a direct link between the Mafia and this phantom lake of oil – about 350,000 non-existent tonnes in volume. Worth some £400 a tonne in EEC production aids, the opportunity was too good to miss. At first the Commission tried to dampen the row with homely speculation about small-scale fiddles run as cottage industries among the peasantry. 'Has the Commission yielded to the mafioso without so much as an inquiry?' asked Brian Hord accusingly in Strasbourg.

The watchdog Court of Auditors had already peered into the depths of the olive oil lake, and found it one massive, glutinous mess of maladministration. Standards for keeping a check on production claims were described as vague and chaotic, with an unhealthy spider's web of connections touching producer organisations and some of Italy's main political parties. This thinly veiled accusation of corruption, involving the massage of output figures to buy votes, sent a shock through the machinery of the Italian state. The Commission itself was slated for sloppy management, failure to pursue control checks rigorously, and allowing the situation to deteriorate virtually unhampered for the best part of a decade.

The Court of Auditors did not dip their legal toes into the oily claims of Mafia involvement: but the sheer scale of the scandal, which shocked even seasoned fraud-watchers in the EEC, left no room for doubt. The Commission's own tame inquiries into Mafia links were dismissed as white-wash by MEPs, particularly since damaging new evidence was already emerging from a mass trial of 400 mafioso suspects in Palermo. A former Mafia boss turned state's evidence and declared that the brotherhood had been lifting money from the CAP for years. Nervous bureaucrats in Brussels were practically mute. An internal report prepared for onward transmission to parliament declared: 'The impact of the Mafia appears weaker than was previously believed.' The Commission's own internal fraud squad sent figures to Strasbourg to suggest that no more than £6 million had been pocketed by the Mafia – which hardly squared with conventional wisdom in Italy that in Naples alone, the local fraternity coined £1 million a week from forging false claims for tomatoes taken off the market and supposedly destroyed to keep prices up. The Mafia employed their own selective methods to deter indelicate probing by outsiders. One senior official from the Court of Auditors, despatched on a mission to Sicily, had his inquiries abruptly terminated when a motor-cyclist knocked him down, breaking both his legs.

The cry to root out 'Mafia thugs' echoed around the parliamentary chamber in Strasbourg. That task ultimately fell to an Italian MEP from the heart of the oldest family's empire, Sicily itself. Pancrazio de Pasquale, a Communist from Palermo, revealed that embezzlement by the Mafia had cost the EEC hundreds of millions of lira and had spilled like an overflowing lake into every area of CAP activity. The figures he produced were startling: 29 billion lira drained away by adulterating wine; another 13 billion lost in one case involving citrus fruit taken off the market; 12 billion centring on a fruit and vegetable fraud in Catania. He said the Italian authorities had uncovered no less than 350,000 'irregular documents' for olive oil and grain. Denouncing a 'conspiracy of silence' in the EEC, Sgr de Pasquale warned: 'To say nothing of the Mafia is purely and simply *omerta* – complicity through silence which allows it to prosper.' He went on to denounce the 'pollution of legal channels by dirty money'. By this means apparently respectable enterprises in Germany allowed their trading interests to be manipulated by 'Calo', a Mafia boss. The Community had become the victim of a vast chain of systematic deception frauds spreading out from southern Italy. The Commission's inquiry he dismissed with the words '*tutto da ridere*' – a vast joke. After a lightning six-day visit, officials described in 'six little pages pompously called a report' how controls should operate, without drawing practical conclusions. 'This attitude reassures the corrupters and the corrupted and it is on this attitude that the Mafia counts.'

The Commission's weak and vacillating response certainly had all the appearance of political cowardice. Agricultural Commissioner Frans Andriessen lamely told the house that even where irregularities were proven, his officials could not prove involvement of the Mafia. He listed a series of screw-tightening and window-closing measures whose marginal relevance stunned MEPs. Yet only ten days previously, the Guardia di Finanza had brought charges against no fewer than 830 people accused of committing frauds at the expense of the European Community, the vast majority involving olive oil, tomato and fruit 'irregularities' in Campania and Sicily. A magistrate had conservatively estimated the amounts involved in the region of £100 million. The Commission's pathetic assessment of a mere £6 million lost in fraudulent manipulation of the CAP over three years sank like a lead balloon.

In the wake of this débâcle, claims and counter-claims flew like arrows at Agincourt. Some newspapers claimed that the Mafia had planted concealed agents inside the Commission itself, with the task of smudging figures and covering tracks. The so-called 'olive tree census' degenerated into high farce. The peasants fiercely resented the EEC's spy in the sky; but cynics suggested that the entire enterprise was doomed from the start, because the Mafia made sure that the pilots flew in concentric circles, repeatedly photographing the same trees to 'make up the numbers'.

Whether the European Commission is guilty of cowardice, as de Pasquale suggested, or straightforward bureaucratic inertia, is of little significance in the final analysis. Without doubt the Mafia and their adherents have extracted a fortune from the European Community and will continue to do so as long as the opportunity is thrust at them. That opportunity is represented by the continued existence of the olive oil 'regime' and the limitless vistas it presents for exploitation. The enlargement of the Community to include Spain and Portugal increased the EEC's production of olive oil by 54.6% at a stroke. The market for oil, which had been progressively stagnating, was instantly flooded, adding yet another pool of excess to the existing surplus foodstocks. By early 1987, the CAP dam was holding back 255,000 tonnes sucked into intervention by the blank cheque policies of Brussels. The pronounced southward tilt in the Community's political geography makes the prospect for practical reform of yet another 'buy-all-you-grow' policy infinitely remote. The 'big four' olive powers – Italy, Spain, Greece and Portugal – will fight change to the last. In the meantime, the Mafia are not only past the gates but in the counting house.

Fraud, as we have seen, is a mostly private enterprise activity. Rarely does it appear to involve the complicity of a member state itself. Yet all diplomatic niceties were abandoned early in 1987 when a senior Commissioner took the unique course of writing to a member state government in unusually blunt terms. The so-called *Alfonsina* Affair went on to rock relations between Brussels and Athens to their foundations. The Greek state international trading company stands accused of blatantly embezzling EEC levies by loading 9,000 tonnes of maize aboard a chartered Panamanian freighter, the *Alfonsina*, in Yugoslavia, then shipping it to Thessalonika before sailing onward to Belgium with false documents describing the cargo as Greek. The Community lost £2.25 million in import dues. Henning Christopherson, the plump and mild-mannered Danish Commissioner in Brussels, spared few feelings in his letter to the Greek government: 'The fraud could have been perpetrated only thanks to the collusion of certain Greek officials and after its perpetration, high-ranking officials of the Greek state issued false documents to cover it up.' In Brussels terms, that is the nearest you can get to a declaration of war. The affair 'posed a threat to the relations of mutual trust between Greece and the Community'. Unless, as Christopherson demanded, everyone involved comes clean, the *Alfonsina* will sail direct to the EEC court at Luxembourg, where the Greeks, who have earned a reputation for playing truancy with EEC regulations, will get another drubbing.

What the incident underlines is the virtual impotence of

EEC institutions in the war against fraud. The Mafia may occasionally have their wings clipped, but carry on again regardless: a few individuals are imprisoned or fined when caught with too much butter in their tarts or devising ingenious recipes to enliven mortadella with horse dung: once in a blue moon, a member state may be pushed into the dock for a ritual wrist-slap. But the disease itself will continue to fester untreated so long as the Community spends £5.9 billion a year on subsidies paid to traders when they shift goods inside and outside the Community. This huge sum now swallows one quarter of the entire EEC budget, and some ten per cent, at best a conservative estimate, is milked away by organised crime. If these border taxes were abolished, then criminal activity which feeds on them would disappear. This is equally the case with the huge sums ladled out for fruit and vegetables removed from the market to re-inflate prices, and the swampy mire of 'processing aids' which in 1980 fuelled a miraculous increase of 80% in Italian production of tomato paste, matched only by a similar record output in France.

Professor Tiedemann stresses that fraud aimed at Community finances is a criminal activity inherent in any planned economic system when the normal control mechanisms of the market system no longer operate. He says: 'A planned economic system with its subsidies and constraints produces a spiral of fraud . . . and a powerful incentive for the establishment of elaborate systems for committing fraud.'

The largely desk-bound enforcement team in Brussels has been overwhelmed by organised exploitation on such a scale – 'it's like shovelling sand in the Sahara with a teaspoon', I was told. The Commission is forced to rely on controls imposed by member states, and the vigilance of lone sentinels like the hero of the Castleblayney trail. In response to a stinging attack on the laxity of fraud controls by the Court of Auditors, the Commission set up 'an interdepartmental committee, whose task will be to explore the possibility of legislation which would ensure that the work of the various national departments monitoring export subsidies becomes complementary and more effective. . .'

When in doubt, set up a committee, then translate its findings into eleven working languages and circulate same for wider discussion. The carousel, meanwhile, rolls happily on.

8

Trade Wars

O Lord, we pray on bended knees
Please make up our deficiencies.
God bless our feeding stuff compounders
And save us from those foreign bounders.

Herbert Andrew, EEC entry negotiator in 1962

Sicco Mansholt's ambition was for a fertile island of self-sufficiency secure from the uncertain world. Although the great agricultural collapse in Africa had yet to come – in the 1950s the continent fed itself adequately, and countries like Ghana and Uganda stored up sound reserves in cocoa and tea – tidal waves of famine swept China and much of Asia at regular intervals. The Soviet Union and its drab empire struggled on grimly with a war diet. The old British Empire – particularly Australia, New Zealand and South Africa – busied the sea lanes with lucrative cargoes of food, much of it bound for British ports. Politically, the world lurched between the various phases of deep-freeze and semi-thaw in super-power relations. In the east the Japanese were on the march again, armed this time with clever calculators and cheap television sets instead of bullets and guns. Individual European economies gulped down lungfuls of the fresh air of free trade but the wider European dream which had seemed so exhilarating only a few years before had dissipated into foggy bureaucratic inertia. The EEC was trapped in the repetitive groove of the common agricultural policy.

In the late 1950s and early 1960s people talked about free trade in the same way that they expressed a pious hope for the afterlife. The British said they longed for it but feared that opening the doors to chilly breezes of unrestricted competition from France and Germany would expose stultified British industry to pneumonia. Two words – full employment – described the principal article of faith for every post-war British government. Few considered that mass employment could be maintained if Britain surrendered protection and joined the EEC. It was always intellectually dishonest to camouflage Britain's European doubts as a dithering obsession with empire: politicians were far more concerned about the state of a clapped-out economy run by union gauleiters and museum-piece middle managers. The question of whether Britain could or should be European was only emotionally transferred to the attachment with the Commonwealth. But free trade there at least suggested some kind of security, even though many of the country's overseas markets were already being mopped up by adept foreign infiltrators.

The United States expressed the same principle in different form, handing out the purple hearts to 'most favoured nations'. The American economy was still coasting on the wartime boost and picking up speed again through the enormous spin-off generated by a huge defence budget. The Japanese were the only ones with a long-term economic plan and they had no belief in free trade whatsoever. The 20-year target set by the Japanese economics ministry to capture control of world trade in advanced electronics worked on the basis of a one-way street which blocked out reciprocal imports. The six nations of the EEC who had made so much of sweeping away all internal barriers as the first stage in constructing a pan-European confederation – Wordsworth's line 'Bliss it was in that dawn to be alive' sums up all the original excitement – instead devoted prodigious energy to maintaining every conceivable frontier obstruction to trade. The Germans particularly saw Europe as an economic colony, and still do. They have long practised their own version of the Japanese one-way street. Thirty years after the signing of the Treaty of Rome, the unlikely figure of Lord Arthur Cockfield, the British EEC Commissioner whom Mrs Thatcher considered had 'gone native', is rated a revolutionary for his optimistic plan to achieve a fully-integrated common market before the end of this century.

But for the British the matter of Europe would not go away. The long debate opened up again the submerged divisions between free traders and protectionists inside the Conservative party and confronted Labour with a challenge it preferred not to face. The Labour party, a political marsupial which developed along quite separate lines from continental social democracy, reached instinctively for isolationism. So Labour's opposition to EEC entry was institutional although the party ultimately broke its back on the issue when the social democrats finally challenged the entrenched Left. For the Tories Europe posed uncomfortable theological questions. When entry was at last seriously attempted, opposition within the Conservative party divided itself more or less evenly along the fissure between free traders (the party's own social democratic rump, with Heath and Peter Carrington as cheer-leaders) and traditional protectionists masquerading as Empire Loyalists. The void between them still exists. Scratch any member of Teddy Taylor's 'European Reform Group' in the House of Commons and you will find protection in the blood. At the Foreign Office, phrases like free trade are a synonym to describe the emergence of the United Kingdom as a respectable continental power. Mrs Thatcher, who instinctively is more at home with the European agnostics, pragmatically keeps a high-heel in both camps – No (as yet) to the EMS, but Yes to the Channel Tunnel.

The great debate over what to do about Europe absorbed

British political energies for the best part of two key decades while British industry continued to advance rapidly to pensionable age. Almost no one noticed what was actually happening to the European Community we could not make up our minds to join. It was slipping effortlessly towards dogged insularity. The world trade seas were getting rough, becoming tempestuous with the onset of the oil crisis in the 1970s. Internal trade was strictly managed while the original Six closed up the hatches to ward off flood from the outside. The CAP, still the only common economic policy, bolstered the prevailing spirit of protection. None of this was unique to Europe. The process was matched all over the globe, as subliminal forces evolved mutually-deflecting tectonic plates of economic activity. Just as the continents had drifted and divided millennia before, so they now altered and changed their positions again to conform with the magma of economic forces moving beneath them. The Soviet Union ruled one such sphere: the United States, which briefly captured Europe during the era dominated by the Truman doctrine, effectively lost it again when the EEC was formed. Britain bumped about uncertainly between the two – many consider that the final attachment is still not clear. There are still people who believe in Atlantis. In the Far East, Japan was well on the way to becoming the dominant regional power, gathering up nations with teeming markets of opportunity, and poised to control China.

The British deluded themselves that membership of the EEC club equalled free trade. In fact, they simply exchanged one intensive form of protection for another. The electorate thought the argument rested on new economic territory – the superficial 'dream topping' of more work and new jobs advocated first by Edward Heath, then subsequently re-served in the European referendum campaign in 1975. Because of the enfeebled state of British industry, most of the jobs were instantly exported across the

Channel. Industrial reconstruction would have to wait for Margaret Thatcher. The Labour party was also seriously in need of reconstruction, which Harold Wilson thought he had achieved by coupling up temporarily with the social democrats to crush the Left in the EEC referendum.

The prospect of the British coming over the water both troubled and excited our new partners. The French fretted that we would break up the common agricultural policy and end their political dominance over Europe (for which the Germans would be truly thankful), while smaller powers, like the Low Countries, expected us to inject a powerful dose of democracy into an organisation already suffering from incipient arthritis. The European Commission flexed its muscles to defend the *ancien régime* of community preference while doing nothing to arrest the slow decay of Europe as an economic force in the world. Instead, the British astonished everyone by arriving in Brussels loaded down with political baggage composed entirely of domestic preoccupations. The socialists behaved rudely, mostly to each other but also to others who wanted to be their friends, while the Tory party went in for high-wire acrobatics which consistently offered the promise of a spectacular fall. The voters, still reluctant to swop the old patriotism for a new one, remained suspicious.

Alone of all the nine member states in the expanded Community (Ireland and the Danes had joined on Britain's coat-tails but the Norwegians had second thoughts and stayed at home), only Britain could seriously lay claim to a world view. France, despite many protestations, has never been a global power, handicapped by the lack of any effective relationship with the United States and an obstinate refusal to create enduring domestic political structures. A fragmentary moment thus existed when the British might have turned Europe in a new direction, tearing down the self-imposed barriers of the CAP, propelling the emerging confederation towards its promised role as an effective third force poised, economically and politically, between the tectonic plates supporting the Soviet Union and the USA. This could only be achieved at the expense of dispensing with regulatory mechanisms like the CAP, which depress trade, and by striking pacts with other dominant regional powers – the Americans, the Japanese in the Far East (first taking the precaution to colonise Japan's client states to secure a good position for ourselves), and then the emerging and important sub-regional powers like India, Australia and Brazil.

None of this happened. It will be to Europe's eternal regret that it did not. What has occurred instead is a slow drift towards economic atrophy inside the Community – we are reaching the limits of expandable trade between the current member states – while Japan has conquered the only available market in the world which really matters – the Far East. Europe's drift has dismayed the United States, spawned serious tensions within NATO, fuelled the fires of isolationism on Capitol Hill and now launched the trans-Atlantic trade wars on the back of the CAP. New figures in 1986 confirmed the deteriorating trend in Community exports to the rest of the world – down ten per cent in value terms between 1985 and 1986, with a sharp fall – 17% – to developing countries.

Britain's entry into the EEC coincided with the world trade depression. These periodic cycles make purblind protectionism irresistible. The struggle for trade quickly pushed Europeans and Americans into high-profile conflict. The collision was fiercely demonstrated in the struggle to control agricultural exports. Each new recruit to the European Community, whilst politically blessed by the USA, also represented the loss of market share to an American economy floating over the dangerous reefs of an enormous budget deficit. Late in 1986, following the accession of Spain and Portugal, the economic cold war turned hot. The immediate cause was the virtual overnight loss of useful American maize exports to both countries. Washington served notice of retaliatory action against 'EEC products' unless the Community agreed to pay compensation and reopen at least part of the lost Iberian market to hard-pressed grain farmers in the Mid West who were accumulating frightening debts. The Americans produced a viciously-targeted hit list threatened with a 200% hike in import tariffs including British gin, Italian pasta, Spanish olives, French Camembert and cognac, Belgian endives, and so on. The American press invented 'the deli war'. *Le Monde* accused the USA – deeply embroiled in the Iranian arms morass – of 'taking commercial hostages'. In Britain, *The Independent* considered it a 'nasty quarrel over who feeds Spanish chickens'.

Grain for Spain is worth a middling $250 million out of America's $53 billion trade with Europe, but what the hostilities really exposed was the USA's festering anger over the EEC's employment of massive subsidies to export mountains, dunes and lakes of surplus food. The Europeans had already been charged with poaching important American food-export markets in North Africa and eastern Europe. Faced with intense pressure from farm belt senators and congressmen, President Reagan (who had already dropped his post-Afghanistan embargo on grain exports to the 'evil empire' behind the Iron Curtain) resolved to prove that he now meant business with trade-stealing Europeans. To stiffen that resolve, the new Democrat majority in Congress flourished the prospect of a fiercely-protective Trade Bill under the President's nose. Major American industries – cars, steel, footwear, machine tools, lumber and, of course, agriculture – had all been clamouring for more protection. That the huge trade imbalance between the USA and the rest of the world is primarily caused by the budget deficit and a superheated dollar is not an argument much of American industry wants to hear: good old-fashioned drawbridges are easier to run-up than budget solutions. So the argument has settled itself on the use of subsidies to lubricate exports. The Europeans packed their 'minister' for external affairs, the Belgian liberal EEC commissioner Willy de Clerq, off to Washington with a warning that Europe would retaliate with lead weights on imports from America on corn, gluten wheat and rice. So the Americans raised the stakes by dragging in subsidies paid by European governments to build the Airbus, the phoenix of the European aerospace industry which had started to eat seriously into Boeing sales.

Bitter salvoes were exchanged across the Atlantic between supposedly friendly powers. Jacques Delors, French president of the European Commission, accused the United States of economic blackmail, and Clayton Yeutter, the US Special Trade Representative, rejoined by saying he would stop 'whole hampers of European food dead in their tracks'. The Russians relished this ugly dispute. A fudged compromise was always inevitable: it took the form of a quota for US grain exporters to continue feeding Spanish chickens which, as *The Economist* declared, meant a victory for the worst type of market protection. If world free trade is the ultimate seamless garment, then bilateral deals are gashes and tears. Two-way deals like that run directly counter to the brief for free-trade negotiators in Geneva to loosen up the binds on world commerce.

Within days of the settlement – Foreign Office ministers in the Commons trumpeted with premature glee that the 'threat' to British gin had been lifted – the EEC and America were back on collision course again. Tit-for-tat trade retaliations were threatened once more when the European Commission revived a dusty old plan to impose a tax on imported oils and fats. This time it was America's turn to censure the EEC for hostile protectionism. As always, the CAP was the villain of the drama. The fats and oils tax resurfaced in the 1987 farm-price package as a way to impose punitive levies on substitute oils used to manufacture butter alternatives like margarine. The food industry in Britain reacted swiftly, warning that the levy would hit the use of vegetable oils right across the consumer index, doubling the cost of raw materials used in bread-making, confectionery and biscuits. The price of margarine might rise by 40%. The Saturday treat of 'fish and chips' by a similar amount. Brussels has always hankered after the levy as a persuasive device to force Europeans into consuming surplus milk. But it would also strike at imports from countries like the United States who are awkwardly large competitors to the EEC's own grossly protected domestic oils-producing industry. International trading laws are supposed to stop the EEC – or anyone else – from slapping on punitive levies to shut out imports. But Brussels proposed to skirt the law by imposing an internal levy, too, believing this would not only camouflage the ulterior protective motive but also create a useful fund to pay for Europe's oils surplus. From the other side of the Atlantic, that looks like more subsidised dumping. The Americans were not fooled.

In just three years from 1983, rapeseed oil gushing from livid yellow pastures (a non-indigenous crop which seriously disfigures the English summer landscape) soared to a Community harvest of 3.2 million tonnes. Sunflower oil kept pace, rising to 2.13 million tonnes. The United Kingdom alone is expected to crush 1.2 million tonnes of rape oil in 1987, double the figure for the previous year. Only the absence of any formal protocol prevents a new addition to the margins of excess imposed by the CAP – a vegetable oil lake. This happens at a time when the bottom has fallen out of the world market for vegetable oils. The European Commission – those Bourbons who have seen everything, yet learnt nothing – will subsidise British farmers to produce rape oil to the tune of £120 million in 1987. European requirements are easily satisfied by recourse to the saturated world market. Self-sufficiency is at work again. The excuse supplied in Brussels is the memory of a short-term crisis in the United States some ten years ago, when the country virtually ran out of soya after a serious crop shortfall and a big surge in Soviet purchases. Lessons like that are never forgotten by the managers of the CAP. Now, as the tides of surplus swell uncontrollably throughout the world, and particularly in Europe, big companies like Unilever have been shedding jobs. Five hundred have already gone in the United Kingdom. The new levy – which would hit EEC producers as well as importers – could only exert more pressure on profit margins by reducing consumption.

Everyone at the Foreign Office performed somersaults. Days after the truce with America in the Spanish grain war – in which Britain backed the EEC against US 'protectionism' – Sir Geoffrey Howe was forced to turn against Brussels. 'This is a hoary old proposal. It has whiskers on it. If you lift up the whiskers, you will find problems not solutions. It is very bad news for consumers and the UK does not support this kind of open protectionism.' The Foreign Secretary did not say, but might have done, that the UK itself now has an oils industry complete with vociferous lobby, another creature of the CAP. Britain was compelled to switch sides in this new phase of the transatlantic trade wars.

The usual posturing and squaring-up before a fight was soon well advanced. Commissioner Andriessen huffed that Washington was over-reacting, failing to appreciate the 'equitable' nature of a tax which hits imports and the home-grown product alike. At a Brussels press conference, he testily rejected accusations that it was 'illogical' to sell butter to the Russians at bargain-basement prices while charging European consumers more for their margarine. 'The question is not very intelligent', he said, 'because the two problems are quite different.' Consumers will be forgiven for failing to see why.

The Commission are trapped as usual by the common agricultural policy. The tax looked desperately necessary to mop up the cost of the oils policy without imposing more strains on the riddled Community budget. It could raise money to shore up the olive oil industry in southern Europe, particularly as the full impact of tending the Spanish and Portuguese olive groves is yet to come. The twelve member states, who always try to look the other way when, like Oliver Twist, the EEC comes asking for more, must ultimately confront an obese budget swollen by excessive farm spending. Most of the 'northern' countries, including Germany and Holland, opposed the oils tax. But the idea will come around again unless the budget is radically reformed or something is done to curb excessive output, particularly of olive oil.

Trade wars with Japan take a different form. The huge explosion in Japanese manufactured imports and the persistent trough of low pressure dominating Europe's ventures in the hi-tech field has bequeathed an excessively-warped trade balance between the two economic powers. The Japanese, exquisitely subtle negotiators, have carefully avoided being lured into a single bilateral pact with the Community. The EEC has been trying for years to push Tokyo into a binding pact, which would almost certainly mean a Community-wide quota system regulating sensitive imports like cars, computers and advanced consumer electronics. The Japanese prefer to pick off the opposition piecemeal. Germany, Italy and France all impose highly-restrictive quota controls on car imports: Britain relies on voluntary restraint, rendered largely meaningless by Japanese penetration of sickly home-based enterprises like Austin Rover. The latest venture is a complete custom-made Japanese car plant in the north-east. Once again, the British are caught hopping from one foot to another. We join our EEC neighbours in loudly deploring Japan for refusing to admit European imports, whilst quietly showing them in by the back door to make cars and computers in the front room. London's subsequent threat to expel Japanese merchant bankers – Britannia girding her loins for a trade war with Tokyo – makes even less sense in this context. With a perfect oriental sense of business acumen, the Japanese then proceed to strike one-off bargains with the Europeans, reducing imbalanced tariffs on strategic commodities like shampoo and chocolate drops. Otherwise sensible people rush about the European Parliament, waving proof that 'tough talking' finally works on Nippon, whilst excitedly threatening a complete embargo to ensure surrender.

The Japanese are of course playing the protectionist game with cynical endurance. They are only momentarily irritated when the French squeeze all their video imports through an Alpine rescue hut manned by a solitary customs officer. Upwardly mobile Europe is firmly hooked on Sony Walkmans and compact discs. And so far as trade barriers are concerned, the Japanese inquire inscrutably: 'What is it that you would actually like to sell us?' This question always wounds, because the Europeans cannot produce a satisfactory answer. The Japanese are filling a vacuum created by European industry which has not so far met the challenge of new consumer technology.

Not that the Japanese are entirely without conscience in face of this one-sided trading relationship. One of Tokyo's most influential newspapers, echoing a fear that Japan's economic resurgence has fuelled latent nationalism, especially among the new samurai of businessmen, recently declared: 'They are the ones who rudely state that Asia is dirty, the Middle East unreliable, the US incompetent, western Europe half-dead and the socialist bloc inefficient.' What the Japanese have done is to reinvent the Greater South East Asia Co-Prosperity sphere – the economic force behind the military reality of the last war. Girt as she is by an ocean of protection, Japan looks vulnerable in only one sensitive sector – agriculture. Japan's food is produced from a small but intensively cultivated area, dosed with lavish subsidies. Rice is three to four times the price it is on the world market. Japanese consumers pay about 60% more for their food than they ought. By forcing Japan into multi-lateral reductions of agricultural subsidies, a path might be sliced through the tariff walls which surround the world's most prosperous nation. Recruits are flooding to the belief that unless this happens, the immense energies of Japan might once again be diverted towards an idea which has disturbingly surfaced again – a 'necessary re-adjustment in the hierarchy of world power to favour Japan', as one leading Japanese political commentator observed.

There is a forum which offers the chance to take out agricultural subsidies as a first step in the process of creating genuinely liberal world trade. That is the new session of GATT (General Agreement on Tariffs and Trade) now under way in Geneva. The new round of discussions at this United Nations related organisation is crucial because farm subsidies are on the table for the first time. Despite powerful opposition from France, the Community reached an accord which (to quote Peter Pooley once again) will allow 'all our warts and our beauty spots – loan rates, dual pricing systems, export boards, special waivers, guarantee systems – the lot' to be thrown in like chips at a casino. All the sacred cows of agriculture are theoretically faced with slaughter if this marks a step on the road to a world free from subsidies. This apparently remarkable conversion is not, however, quite so impressive as it seems. For a start, the Community is on poor ground by pretending that its limited tinkering with problem fringes of the CAP can be squared with a trade-strangling oils and fats levy. And as Commission president Jacques Delors told

Euro MPs in Strasbourg, the farm policy itself is not available for execution.

Seasoned economic commentators – and many cynics – think that GATT will take little more than a fretsaw to prune the sprawling jungle of world farming subsidies. Their sheer scale in global terms is truly awesome. Geoffrey Miller, a radically-inspired Australian crusader for genuine reform, has demonstrated how massive subsidy programmes are crucifying countries like his own which depend on agriculture for 36% of its export earnings. The Americans easily top the bill – they will spend $30 billion of taxpayers' money – $700 per family – on farm support in 1987. Two-thirds of all direct payments to American farmers will go to those who are already far wealthier than the average citizen. The really lucky ones will get $1 million each. If American cows had bank accounts, they would all be earning interest, since consumers will feed each of them $835 this year. Grain stocks in the United States have now grown to equal two years of total world trade. The EEC sins on only a slightly reduced scale. The cost of the CAP is heading in dollar equivalent for a $23-billion peak in 1987, and when all the hidden national top-ups are counted in, this will mean a charge of $900 on every family from the Tagus to the Rhine. As in America, the rich will get richer, since a quarter of Europe's farmers with the biggest output will drain 75% of all farm support, roughly $9,000 for each of them. No wonder some could scarcely trust their ears after a radio broadcast in Britain, in which Michael Jopling blithely declared that farmers should be pleased with the government's fearless determination to take the axe to public expenditure.

The oldest ploy in the world of international forums is to agree to talk about specific issues, but not quite yet. In order to drag both the Europeans and the Americans kicking and screaming to the GATT table, it was essential to fudge up a compromise which looks like straight talking on farm

126

subsidies yet secures the avenue of retreat at the same time. When the world's two largest subsidy-sinners – the USA and the EEC – met face-to-face at Geneva, they agreed on an expanded 'initial phase' to consider American demands for a total phasing out of farm export subsidies – the means by which unwanted surpluses are dumped on world markets. This would chop nearly a third of the fat from the CAP but leave nothing in the kitty to unload present and future surpluses. In agricultural terms, this is the equivalent of the zero option which another set of negotiators are discussing elsewhere in Geneva. The Americans and Europeans are committed only in the vaguest terms to real talking in 1988 once the cosmetic 'initial phase' is out of the way. All this stage-setting was necessary to ensure the essential participation of the French, still sulking because they were the principal losers in the grain wars with the United States. Germany also behaved badly at the preliminary talks.

Little New Zealand, meanwhile, has claimed for itself the cloak of purity. The country's Labour government (right-wing at the cash register, left-wing on nuclear weapons) has commenced a series of remarkable and almost completely unreported liberal reforms of the economy. These include the virtual abandonment of agricultural subsidies. The government concluded with straightforward honesty that it could not afford them and then took the only possible course. Some excitable headlines spoke of 2,000 farmers going bankrupt and others driving sheep over cliffs. It is true that the lamb price farmers receive has dropped by two-thirds. Incomes have fallen by around 40% and around 16% of New Zealand's dairymen are facing what the dairy board agrees is 'a very difficult time'. There were anguished demonstrations outside parliament in Wellington. Farm ministers in Europe like Michael Jopling served this up as proof of the dread prospect to be faced by EEC farmers if they were unhitched from intravenous money.

But other observers tell a different story. Land values in New Zealand have fallen, but not collapsed, and this has made it easier for people to get on the land instead of leaving it – the inverse of Europe's problem. Lamb exports are buoyant, with new markets in Japan and elsewhere in the Far East. A brand new rapid-freeze plant is positive investment for the future. The country's main farmers' union speaks of a rapid switch to alternative crops, like deer-farming, and a big shift towards quality instead of quantity, both of which are supposed to be major targets of the EEC's cumbrous efforts to redirect the CAP. With a clean face and a subsidy-free smile, New Zealand therefore has every right to accuse the EEC of using dirty subsidy tricks to filch important butter contracts with the Soviet Union.

If the Americans and Europeans cannot make constructive progress at Geneva, present transatlantic upsets will look like squalls compared to the storm to come. The Europeans are getting sloppy with their thanks to the Americans for sending over a garrison of 350,000 men to keep the peace in Europe these last 40 years. Taking the American commitment for granted is beginning to annoy many influential thinkers on Capitol Hill. It is becoming increasingly hard to maintain support for existing troop levels in Europe without some clear demonstration of elasticity by Europeans on farm export subsidies. The trade-and-troops link is being heavily underscored by Henry Kissinger, who has taught for years that Europe is becoming complacent over the security pact with the USA and could do with a sharp reminder on fair deals for all. Too many Europeans – including highly-placed individuals in the European Commission – are inclined to shrug off American warnings as bluster at best, blackmail at worst. They also pointedly ignore the probability that in the next century the United States is more likely to be a Pacific power than a continuing force in the Atlantic. The common agricultural policy is grit in the eye of the Atlantic Alliance: a failure to pick it out could lead to blindness when all Europeans desperately need the clearest possible view of the future.

9

A Cap the World Will Not Wear

'In the developed world, malnutrition has
been slowly eliminated. It remains now
confined to the developing world.'

Professor David Grigg, The World Food Problem

When Bob Geldof visited the European Parliament in
Strasbourg in 1986, he said that what the EEC really needed
was a good dose of emetic. A few pompous souls reacted
sourly. After all, the European Community had been
feeding the hungry long before an Irish songsmith took up
a folk crusade for the victims of the Ethiopian catastrophe.
The EEC can with some justice flourish a moral conscience
by pointing to a massive aid programme and a long history
of moving mountains to the famine-stricken countries of
Africa; but Geldof's inspiration was to release the long-
smouldering resentment created by the man-made excess
of the common agricultural policy, and the vulgar contrast
it offers with blighted lands where perfectly innocent
people starve to death on cue for nightly television broad-
casts. The first BBC reports from Ethiopia unleashed that
previously unfocused resentment and Geldof caught the
tide of outraged public opinion at its flood. Band Aid raised
millions but the anger it engendered was always far more
important than the money. Geldof punctured the cocoon of
complacency which allowed the CAP to manufacture
mountains of excess for pampered Europeans while the
fate of human beings elsewhere conjured back urgent and

disturbing visions of the victims of Nazi tyranny. The minstrel from Dublin dragged out these subliminal terrors and waved them under the noses of EEC bureaucrats and Euro MPs. Many of them bitterly resented a populist equipped with designer stubble and a rich line in adjectives invading a private domain. The combination of pity and a desperate sense of frustration felt by ordinary people did not simply evaporate, as it had done so often before: it spilled over to fuel a new political debate which centred on the smug complacency surrounding a system based on greed instead of need.

It is too easy to believe that the surpluses produced in the European Community can simply be dumped in the Third World to relieve famine, poverty and intense social deprivation. And to be fair, the EEC's food aid policy was always intended as a fire brigade to meet instant and unpredicted disaster. The dangers of employing food aid as an almost permanent tribute have been well-rehearsed. Inevitably, severe dislocation of local markets swiftly follows, agricultural patterns are disrupted and in some cases, destroyed. Recipient countries soon grow to dislike charity recycled from former colonialist donors, which offends the sensibilities of independent nations and raises the old ghost of economic imperialism. Some commodities – like the cheese once sent to Biafra – are clearly inappropriate. Yet many Euro MPs jumped to their feet during debates on the latest African tragedy to introduce the fatally attractive argument that Europe's surpluses are an essential insurance for the world's hungry. As the World Bank's latest essay on developing countries effectively proves, the opposite is true. The EEC's enormous excess in food production flattens world price levels, inflicting great damage on frail, emerging economies where there is as yet no effective alternative to agriculture of some kind as the principal exchange-earner. Whilst the EEC is the world's largest importer of food products (and 60% of these originate in

131

the Third World), they are nearly all products which cannot be grown in a European climate – such as tea, coffee and tropical fruit. In return the Community also ranks as the second largest exporter of food – cereals, sugar, dairy products and meat – which are both grown and consumed in developing countries. So the Community is in the contradictory position of being both purchaser and competitor in the developing world. Market distortion is further complicated by the EEC's determination to supply as much as it can from its own internal market. The consequences ricochet around the globe as countries which have become dependent on supplying the European market attempt to keep pace with the twists and contortions in EEC food policy.

The great tapioca crisis in Thailand serves as a precise example. In natural form tapioca comes from a tuber – cassava is the generic name – which looks rather like a large dahlia corm. Twenty years ago, Europe discovered this staple Far East vegetable as a cheap and nutritious supplement to the diet of pigs and cattle when mixed with a little soya and ground into pellets. The huge expansion in German and Dutch pork production was largely made possible by the tapioca plantations of Thailand, where the trade rapidly assumed the proportions of a major export earner. The Thais were soon collecting some £900 million a year, second only to rice as the principal traditional crop. The roads from north-east Thailand (where little else will grow except tapioca) down to the wharves at Bangkok were jammed with thousands of lorries employed on a constant merry-go-round. Such was the mayhem on the quays that people actually drowned in the mad scramble to load up freighters bound for Europe. But the French government had begun to complain in Brussels that every tonne of tapioca landed in Rotterdam pushed another tonne of French barley off the market. The cheap tapioca flooding in from Thailand as a cereal substitute for cattle breeders was denounced as a violation of the EEC's standard credo of self-sufficiency. In no time at all, the bureaucrats imposed tough import quotas which immediately trimmed four million tonnes of tapioca from the Thais' annual export total.

Professor Amma Siamwalla, who heads Thailand's rural development programme, says that the north-east of the country became a disaster area virtually overnight as the tapioca exports dwindled away. No one in Thailand could comprehend why bureaucrats in a far-off European city had suddenly decided to cut off the flow of life-giving trade. 'The moral element in this argument is why should people in Brussels bully a small nation like ours when they are afraid to tackle other super-powers, like the Americans, on their contribution to the world cereal surplus.' The decision was apparently taken without any reference whatsoever to the fragile nature of the Thai economy, or how the collapse of a vital activity employing hundreds of thousands of peasant farmers might induce political may-hem in its wake. The Thais have hovered for years on the brink between dictatorship and democracy, with 16 coups, successful and botched, in the past 55 years. A major insurgency by Communist rebels continues to crackle through the northern highlands. Next door the Cam-bodians stand bitter testimony to the fate of small, de-stabilised countries. No domino yet perhaps, but if what passes for democracy in Thailand (a sort of benign military oligarchy) is to survive, then Europe should offer the helping hand of trade.

Perversely, practically every pig farmer in Europe would agree. The EEC's hasty lock-out of tapioca, artificially contrived to force higher consumption of European sur-pluses, has hit them where it hurts most, in the pocket. The pig industry gets no support whatsoever from the common agricultural policy and for years has been trapped in a recurring cycle between boom and bust. Even well-organised, industrial producers like the Danes suffer from the soaring cost of EEC grains which they must feed to their animals instead of cheap imported substitutes like tapioca. They are thus crushed by the lavishly-subsidised barons of the home-grown grain industry. This is an old split in agriculture – in Britain the conflicting pressures may wreck the main national farmers' union – and it has led to powerful demands from the pigmen for the key to the door of the overflowing granaries. So far, the EEC Commission refuses to hand it over, whilst only too keen to dump the grain surplus on the eager Russians at knock-down prices denied to the producers of European pork. The final mad twist came after the tapioca quotas were managed with total ineptitude: the EEC was forced to acquire a 'tapioca mountain' when importers lavishly exceeded their quotas.

Tapioca is on a list with molasses (a by-product of sugar), citrus pulp, copra-cake (from coconuts), fishmeal and maize germ (what remains from the oil extraction process). All take their place on Europe's menu for animal feeds. Some 36 million acres are planted in developing countries to feed the ruminants of the EEC. As the world's largest purchaser of animal feeds, the Community has the power to make or break an economy overnight. Between 1970 and 1982, imports multiplied four-fold. When the 'marriage contract', the CAP, was negotiated in the early 1960s, no one seriously contemplated striving for self-sufficiency, particularly since there was no shortage of grass. What changed the picture dramatically was the emergence of grain surpluses. Cheap substitutes are attractive to live-stock farmers but do not suit the managers of the CAP so long as the EEC is stuck with the problem of storing and dumping grain. The entrenchment of self-sufficiency has in turn led to enormous expansion in subsidies for crushing oils (£170 per metric tonne in the case of rapeseed), a figure which is now rapidly expanding to consume 6% of the total CAP budget. Traditional sources of supply – Pakistan, Mexico, the Sudan, Indonesia and Peru among them – are watching nervously as the Community moves remorse-lessly towards an insular goal of home supply. When the quota blight struck the Thai cassava plantations, Brussels sent a social compensation cheque for £32 million – far less than the £100 million a year lost from natural resource-building exports. Countries like Malaysia who regard the Community as a fickle and selfish trading partner have warned that Europe's march to exclusivity will cost her dear in retaliatory strikes against manufactured imports. Brussels used to regard this as an idle threat, until the day when first Brazil and then Peru refused to pay interest on vast accumulations of debt acquired from international banks. Yet despite these warning signs the European Commission persisted with proposals to tax imports of oils from some of the world's most impoverished and impecunious nations. And while the Pacific gradually becomes a dependency of Japan, Europe's share of trade with six key countries in the ASEAN (Association of South East Asian Nations) grouping has sunk to a miserable 2.6%.

In Brussels, the EEC's external affairs commissioner, Willy de Clerq, thinks that the 'aims and fundamental mechanisms of the CAP cannot be called into question'. In Argentina, that is read as a message without hope. Eighteen years ago, Europe bought nearly fifty per cent of all the country's exports, especially meat. By 1984 the figure had slumped by half. A third of the meat trade was decimated. The Argentinians reckon that CAP subsidies have robbed them of markets worth about a billion dollars in the last two years alone, including markets in Egypt, Israel and the Soviet Union where they were elbowed out by the EEC's aggressive policy of dumping surpluses. Since many Argentinian farmers now find it pointless to produce beef at prices which hardly repay the cost of the feed, the government has been forced to resort to the humiliating coals-to-Newcastle operation of buying chunks from the EEC's frozen beef stores. During this time Argentina has shot up to fourth position in the international debtor league, owing some $47 billion which are unlikely ever to be repaid, certainly so long as natural export markets are asset-stripped by the very countries whose banks sold her the debt in the first place. All this is happening to what the World Bank cites as one of the world's 'most natural farming countries'. Of course other factors are at work: Argentina's remaining food exports would be worth much more were it not for a long history of incompetent administration, high-octane inflation and military adventurism. Nevertheless, slow and deliberate exclusion from crucial export markets consigns what should be a rapidly developing country to the regions of little hope.

Until the early 1950s the global food market was almost in balance. Developing countries had acquired a dominant share, well over 50%, of all food exports. The next two decades were marked by the development of rigorous protectionist policies in America and the EEC. This was the origin of the world debt problem. The poorer countries watched helplessly as their slice of the cake grew progressively smaller, shrinking to 30% by 1980, now down to 27% and still falling. An ominous side-effect – observed but ignored – was the decline of the developing countries' ability to pay for food and essential industrial imports with the natural wealth they used to generate in field and plantation. As one economy followed the next into an economic nose-dive, there were few resources to develop alternative crops to those like jute, cotton, sisal and wool which had been hit by synthetic replacements or shifts in demand. Population growth, particularly in Africa, made it difficult to grow food supplies for home production and at the same time raise something to sell for cash on the world market. Malnutrition brought on by climatic change – as in the countries fringing the southern Sahara – and endemic political unrest in others – Ethiopia, the Sudan, Angola and now Mozambique – contributed to the further dislocation of food supply patterns. Each turn of the protectionist screw in Brussels or Washington reduces the room for manœuvre, while the ranks of those countries which are on the debt rack and cannot or will not pay what they owe lengthens inexorably.

Apologists for the CAP often like to say that what it takes freely with one hand, it generously returns with the other. They base this exaggerated claim on the benefits which are supposed to flow from signing up with a special club whose members are among the smallest and poorest countries in the world. These are the 66 participants who currently belong to the Lomé pact, which in turn guarantees them a degree of privileged access – on the 'most favoured nation' basis – to one of the richest marketplaces in the world. At least, that is the elegant theory. In reality, such preferences as do exist for agricultural produce are effectively rigged against the club of 66. There is one small sector for temperate-grown crops which are also encouraged by the CAP. This matters little to the Lomé states, who are mostly in the business of balmy tropical produce. More promising is the unrestricted access for those products – sugar excepted – since they present no obvious or unwelcome problems of competition for European farmers. However, since similar promises have also been extended to other countries outside the Lomé special relationship, the apparent advantage is not quite as compelling as at first it seems. Profit margins are limited and there is little prospect of winning a significant new slice of the market. Finally, there is a special class containing rum, bananas, beef, rice and of course sugar, where quotas and controls of various kinds intrude.

From my own experience of sitting on a joint committee which links the European Parliament and the Lomé states, I would say that almost all the developing countries disliked the 'Uncle Tom' nature of the bond with the EEC. Most of all they were upset by what they considered arbitrary controls on staple exports like sugar. When the talking starts, the Europeans have all the clout and the small supplicant powers none whatsoever. The World Development Report for 1986 concurred with suspicions that the economic minnows in Lomé were getting a raw deal from their big brothers in the EEC. 'It is possible that all the Lomé Convention has achieved is to change the direction of world trade, without increasing it, while adding to transport costs.' In return for this highly quantifiable reward, the Lomé countries are frozen into a pact with the EEC from which they dare not escape. The only obvious beneficiaries are the shipping companies, who haul sugar from the Caribbean across the Atlantic, only to re-export it promptly again, whilst similarly discharging excess beet sugar from the EEC on to world markets which are already swamped by the sheer volume of over-production. It is estimated that the waste involved in shunting unwanted sugar around the globe now totals around $42 billion a year.

The Lomé pact's close cousin is the Caribbean Basin Initiative, born in 1983, which gave 27 island states in the Caribbean duty-free access for many of their products to the United States. In return, these backyard mini-states were pressured into certain changes in economic and taxation policy which offered attractive potential for the USA. At the time, it looked like a precautionary two-way bet should the Europeans finally decide to wind up the drawbridge. In practice, the trade benefits are entirely one-sided. Sensitive items like textiles, clothing, footwear, canned tuna and petroleum are all excluded: sugar and beef, as usual, labour beneath special protocol, which means the amount of sugar the Caribbean countries can get into America has consistently fallen. And in any case, barely had Uncle Sam proferred a helping hand than it was promptly withdrawn again. The farm lobby pressured Congress into passing the Food Security Act which dictates automatic reductions in basic commodity imports, like sugar, should home producers be seriously threatened by low-cost competitors, particularly those who happen to be on the doorstep. Protection is like a weed: stamped out in one place, it soon re-establishes itself in another.

Strangely enough, this is not the product of a concerted conspiracy by the rich against the poor. It follows from one department of state in Brussels or Washington defending its own localised vested interest against intruders. Traditionally, the aid-and-trade fraternity are political lightweights, except at times when public attention is crudely arrested by dramatic media exposure of severe deprivation in what the analysts kindly describe as 'downstream economies'. When the first great post-war famines swept through the African continent and wide areas of Asia, the need for aid programmes assumed tactical significance. The Americans were the first to spot the trick of tying up aid parcels with political string. A special law passed in 1954 set up a worldwide grain disposal programme, firmly hitched to the expansion of American interests on the back of the steadily-increasing US cereal harvest. The preamble was refreshingly frank. The new law would 'expand international trade among the United States and friendly nations, make maximum efficient use of surplus agricultural commodities in furtherance of the foreign policy of the United States and facilitate the expansion of foreign trade in agricultural commodities produced in the United States. . .'

This explicit link between surplus disposal and American power-broking would be readily exploited today if the Soviet Union were itself able to compete in the global aid game by exporting surpluses: but the Russians have been forced into sullen silence by their own overwhelming need to import American grain. The United States is still the largest food aid donor – more than fifty per cent of the world total in 1985, followed by the EEC (30%), with Australia, Canada and Japan making up the rest. The Communist bloc is conspicuous by its absence. The value of food sent to more than a hundred recipient countries is now approaching $3 billion annually, a major stake in the total volume of world food trade. So massive is this trade that for many years it virtually institutionalised the production of surplus products like grain and skimmed milk powder. The argument that they would always be required to feed the poor and needy appeared deceptively valid.

From 1985 onwards, when farm production in both the USA and the EEC shot up by unprecedented proportions, making nonsense of soaring budget appropriations for agriculture, people began to talk about the unhealthy side-effects of legalised dumping on delicate economies. In practice, it is almost impossible to be sure that the food is even directed at those who most require it. Egypt, for example, gets about twenty per cent of all cereal aid, although the country is well above minimum nutritional standards. The deciding factor here is blatantly political: a moderate regime might easily be threatened if bread prices were allowed to rise realistically. In contrast, the impoverished west African republic of Togo, which is quite unable to overcome an inbuilt food deficit, gets only about 6% of the grain donated to mostly healthy Egyptians. The Americans and the EEC have also quarrelled seriously over grain exports to countries like Egypt, which the USA considers its own captive market.

Shipments of food also run into many other problems. In countries like the Sudan and Ethiopia, where transport is chaotic and further handicapped by distortions of war and huge refugee movements, much of the food is never distributed at all, or falls into the wrong hands. Only about two-thirds of the food aid sent to the Sudan left the ports in 1984–85. In Somalia, it is thought that about thirty per cent of recent emergency aid was lost during handling at the dockside. Consignments sometimes take so long to arrive that monsoons destroy roads before distribution can start. By the time it is handed out, the pressing urgency may have passed, causing severe distortion to the local economy.

This happened in Kenya, which in 1983 hit a cyclical shortage of maize and then found aid arriving in huge quantities twelve months later when the home-grown harvest had caught up again with a record crop. Bewildered Kenyan farmers saw prices collapsing and the government was forced to export maize from its own bulging granaries at a loss.

Too often, food aid discourages local production, forcing prices down and driving farmers away from the land. Countries then get trapped in the grip of virtual permanent dependence on imports. This was realised as long ago as 1961, when the United Nations and the FAO (Food and Agriculture Organisation) set up a joint programme to manage food aid. The inspiration behind the initiative was to co-ordinate emergency aid on a planned basis, so that fragile economies could avoid being swamped while still guaranteed immediate help in case of famine or failure of the rains. Nearly thirty years later, only a quarter of all food aid shipments are handled under the UN programme, which remains severely hampered by persistently chaotic distribution systems and the lack of any effective early-warning system to identify a crisis in creation.

A recent report by Oxfam observed that no one starting from scratch today would invent food aid on its present scale. And Britain's overseas development minister, Chris Patten, moved quickly to decouple the link between getting rid of expensively-produced surpluses and food shortages in the Third World. He preferred to offer potential recipients a choice between aid in the form of food or cash to reconstruct domestic agricultural output. In the EEC, the awkward division of responsibility for food aid between two directorates – including the hard-pressed manager of the subsidy-ridden CAP – stands as a serious obstacle to sensible reforms on a European scale. Oxfam came out powerfully against the use of aid to justify the EEC's swollen agricultural budget and concluded that it 'should only be used sparingly and with great care'. The best way to help the poor, it concluded, was gradually to build up their purchasing power on the world market.

Oxfam was not alone in noting the dichotomy between an EEC food aid budget of £442 million a year and a quite conflicting set of policies, mounted by the same organisation, which effectively conspire against any opportunity by weak countries to win a more equitable share of world trade. At the heart of this conflict is the common agricultural policy, whose obsession with self-sufficiency in Europe is expensive and damaging to the Third World. European farmers continue to produce rapeseed oil at £700 a tonne, while the Indonesians can turn out the same quantity of palm oil for £150. Instead of seizing on this differential to hold prices down, the European Commission proposes a fresh injection of discrimination, by proposing a tax which would strike hardest at those low-cost exporters, like Indonesia, who are struggling to maintain a hold on their corner of the market.

The agricultural decline of Africa, that colossus of under-development, has run unchecked for the best part of 25 years, despite development programmes exported from Brussels, Washington and the aid factors at the UN headquarters in New York. Huge, still sparsely-populated, afflicted by droughts and tinder-dry soil, Africa is hooked on charity. Yet there are those who think a green revolution, such as that which transformed Bangladesh and the Indian Punjab, might be achieved. One of them is Norman Borlaug, whose work in Asia won him a Nobel Prize. His strategy is to select the staple crops – in Africa these are maize, sorghum and millet – and project them right to the front stage under optimum conditions to control weeds, moisture and predatory pests. Borlaug considered that if one or two pilot countries (the Sudan and Ghana ranked as first choice) could be persuaded to take on the experiment, then eager villagers would soon pick up the challenge to feed themselves. Borlaug reckons the cost of a five-year trial at around $5 million per country. So far he has managed to interest only a Japanese philanthropist, but nevertheless a small programme has begun, admittedly with a scientific team numbering precisely five – a platoon in the vast army of aid administrators who populate Africa.

Borlaug's self-help concept is politically unfashionable because it is lightweight, portable and user-friendly – in other words, entirely the opposite of the lumbering aid machines which rumble around Africa. In Asia, it worked: for Africa, it is tailor-made. But the Borlaug philosophy requires no grubby touting for vast aid budgets on which the great pyramid of political side-deals and jobs for the boys can rest. It also renders completely redundant the concept of Europe as a granary for a hungry continent.

The EEC shares with the United States the lack of any overall strategy for the Third World (although America is a good deal more generous than the Europeans in buying manufactures from developing countries – 63% of all they sell, compared to a niggardly 23%). The result is the frighteningly unequal relationship between the developed countries with their subsidised food output and the politically-impotent outsiders who have barely set foot on the ladder of development. Susan George, of the Institute of Policy Studies in Washington, prescribes some new variation on the post-war Marshall Plan which paid for much of the reconstruction in Europe. What the US gained from that act of generosity was a set of guaranteed trading partners in a swiftly recharging European economy. Selfish, perhaps, but the Americans simply did not trust the ability of the Europeans to get out of the fix by themselves. A weak and politically-decentralised Europe could only harbour more trouble. The argument looks just as good today if the developing world is exchanged for war-broken Europe. 'It is the interests of the rich countries that Third World countries should get richer too,' Susan

George argues. Professor David Harvey, of Reading University's department of agriculture, has the same idea and takes it further to suggest a straight switch of all the subsidies invested in EEC farming – about $17,000 million a year – direct to the Third World. But regretfully he concludes: 'Of course this requires a degree of co-operation which seems beyond the bounds of possibility.'

10

A Study in Scarlet

'Ireland's fate in the EEC is to be a permanent
lapdog, a permanent beggar. That is bad for us
and bad for the EEC.'

Raymond Crotty, Ireland in Crisis

1986 was a year in which the fortunes of the Irish edged
dangerously close to the point of collapse. The cheerless
general election early in 1987 took place against a wintry
background fringed by lowering clouds of economic ruin.
The morbid statistics of failure which besiege this small
country on the periphery of the European Community offer
little prospect of recovery. The Irish economic miracle, if it
ever existed, is over. Government expenditure is now
running £2 billion a year ahead of revenue, fuelling a
national debt which has reached the fantastical heights of
£22 billion, £7000 for every man, woman and child in the
country. More than a quarter of a million are now unemployed, almost 20% of the workforce, the highest rate of
jobless in the EEC. The immediate casualties are the young.
Almost half of Ireland's 3.5 million people are under 25 and
the scale of their flight from this benighted land might
depopulate the entire country in the closing years of the
20th century. The saddest Irish exports are now youth and
talent. In January alone, the American Embassy in Dublin
was swamped with 250,000 visa applications – a stunning
7% of the population, equivalent to the population of Cork
decamping all at one go. More than 31,000 went to America

in 1986 alone, to join at least 200,000 immigrants the authorities believe have already passed the Statue of Liberty illegally in the past five years – driven from their native land by poverty and desperation. But emigration is no longer a passport to paradise. 'In the old days you just picked up a boat for three or four quid and got the hell out of it,' one journalist observed. 'But there are three million unemployed in Britain now, and the Irish can't just walk into jobs like they used to 30 years ago.'

Ireland looks and feels like a country too feeble to recover from a potentially terminal malaise. Dublin exudes the air of imminent evacuation. There are beggars in O'Connell Street, wild teenagers have turned tumbledown ware-houses into lawless ghettos. Magical potions the politicians used for years to work their spells on polling day now raise hollow laughs instead of courage. For the first time since independence, Ireland has no sense of future. A group of Irish friends, long since 'over the water', remarked to me recently that when they return home for holidays, they find it unsettling to hear old acquaintances and relatives who stayed behind preoccupied with gloomy talk of death and funerals. And Ireland itself looks like the next candidate for the wake.

The contemporary crisis is beginning to equal the potato famine of the 1840s, which almost drained the country in the first great stampede of emigration to the New World. The trough into which the economy has now sunk is deeper than any since the depression which followed the debilit-ating civil war of the 1920s. The hardest squeeze is in the countryside, where, since Ireland remains essentially a pastoral economy, about one-fifth of the population lives and works. Ireland is thus entirely hostage to the future of the common agricultural policy. The CAP has not proved a gentle guardian so far. After fourteen years of membership of the EEC, Ireland has one-third fewer farmers, 15 times more agricultural debt and fewer people at work in a prime industry than at any time since the 18th century. Nearly 100,000 workers, a third of the entire workforce, have deserted the land.

Farming has always been a hard business in Ireland, so difficult that the uncertainties induced a powerful dread of debt. In part this flowed from a deep-seated reaction against the old absentee aristocracy, whose mansions survive as hotels or disintegrating rookeries for ghosts and bad dreams. The industry was also traditionally under-nourished and technically deficient. For all these reasons, farm debt was almost non-existent twenty years ago. By 1970, it was still only £80 million. Now it is practically £2000 million, on which the interest payments alone consume some £200 million a year. When Ireland – a country with virtually no natural raw materials to exploit – plunged into the European Community in 1973, she was encouraged to believe that 'green oil', the produce of the countryside, would transform her economic expectations. The years of farm boom have now led instead straight to bankruptcy and she ranks along with Greece and Portugal, those other pauper states of the EEC.

There is a groundswell of opinion in Ireland which sees the Community as a trap. 'The land fit for farmers' promised by a bonanza from the CAP and ruthlessly exploited by a succession of indifferent politicians when the going was good, has instead ushered in a new wave of rural depression. Indigenous industrial ventures like textiles and shoe-making have always been labour intensive to mop up unemployment. This exposes Irish industry to crushing competition on two exposed fronts – first from the more efficient and better organised industrial units in other EEC countries, and again from low-cost imports sent into the Community by Third World competitors. Another bruising factor is the wildly over-valued Irish pound, the punt, which has scraped along the bottom of the European

Monetary System ever since Ireland abrogated the currency link with Britain. Trying to keep the punt even remotely on a course with the German Deutschmark was described to me by a senior Irish diplomat in Brussels as 'rather similar to the consequences of fitting a jet engine to a paper kite'.

Ireland joined the EEC principally because she appeared to be left with no alternative once her largest trading partner, Britain, decided to take the plunge. This serves only to underline the view of some economists that Ireland is Europe's only capitalist colony. True, not a few perceived a heaven-sent opportunity at last to break free from the grip of the British, but the prospects for agriculture did seem appealing. Farmers had already been doing their sums and their calculations produced wild excitement in the Irish countryside. Grossly inflated guaranteed prices – set at German levels – promised to transform Irish agriculture.

This argument turned out to be wholly defective. The heavyweight regime of the CAP also imposed huge increases in input costs like cattle feed. And Irish farmers, eager to make hay in this bright new sunshine, forgot all their traditional reluctance to borrow money and rushed off to the banks to buy new and better equipment to squeeze the best from the land. But the banks were chary of lending to the crofters in regions like the deep south-east – 'one-cow country' as they call it in Dublin – and the CAP mostly benefited those who were already big, or about to get bigger. The fact that the CAP had already demonstrated a pronounced tendency to drive small farmers from the land was barely noticed in those heady days of expansion. Also tucked under the carpet were the unpleasant facts about the Irish economy in general, along with the well-known effect of the CAP on any country where low incomes are the norm. Those in the low pay bracket in Ireland spend around 40% of their income on food. As the CAP boosted food prices upwards, they were hit most. Ireland also suffers from a peculiar inversion of revenue-raising, which means that industrial workers subscribe virtually all the national tax income and farmers practically nothing. Those in unattractive poorly-paid industrial jobs were squeezed between soaring taxes and food prices. Here is the origin of today's rush to evacuate a country trapped in a remorseless downward spiral of national expectation.

After the first big spurt in farm incomes immediately following EEC accession, Irish farmers were soon dismayed to discover that the CAP behaved more like a roller-coaster than a permanently-ascending escalator. The initial boost in 1974 was followed by sharp decline, a recovery lasting until 1978, and then slump for two more years. A modest recovery started only to be blown off course by two years of unusually bad weather, even by soggy Irish standards. Professor Sheehy of University College, Dublin, suggests that in the five years to 1985, prices paid to Irish farmers fell overall by 31.6% – by far the largest single reduction throughout the EEC. He wrote: 'If the Commission had declared in 1977 that it proposed to cut prices by this amount, nobody would have believed them. But it has happened.' There was a case, he argued, for the EEC to explain why it allowed such selective damage to be inflicted on one of the poorest states in the Community. Charles Haughey, returned to office as prime minister early in 1987, may have been thinking along similar lines when he indicated that the time had come to 're-negotiate' – a word always received with a considerable chill in Brussels – the terms of Irish membership of the EEC. The prospects for any degree of success are not encouraging. When Irish negotiators looked for compensation for a notably severe farm income decline which followed the punt's entry into the European Monetary System, the results were decidedly meagre. A prominent farm leader said that only 'the lucky bags' did well out of it. Once again, the CAP favoured Goliath rather than David.

The backbone of Irish farming has always been the beef and

dairy industry. In normal circumstances, Ireland is a stockfeed importer. The catch here is that while the CAP in the early years rejuvenated and transformed the dairy sector, the explosion in the size and cost of the grain harvest struck Ireland like a revolving door from the opposite direction. Higher feed costs are gloomy news for a nation of livestock dependents. As Professor Sheehy succinctly puts it, 'The price of cereals in the EEC determines the value of grass in the Irish agricultural economy.' And now there are new blows. The desperate need to curb the Community's excessive milk production has spawned the quotas which artificially restrain output. Yet Ireland's dairy farmers, many of them desperately over-borrowed, are thirsty for more output and new markets in order to win the survival game. Because the CAP has virtually colonised the Irish economy, impotent governments in Dublin are forced to the reality that they have swopped one form of colonial dependence for another. 'Independence' looks like a sham, thrown away for the fairy gold of the CAP.

The irony is that Ireland stands the risk of being trapped yet again by progressive reform of the CAP. 'More of the same' – the extension of quotas and gradual erosion of price support – will depress the farm economy even further, banishing yet more farmers from land they can no longer afford to work, accelerating the process of rural depopulation. A radical shift in the opposite direction, towards less intensively protected agriculture and the chilly breezes of market forces, will strip away even the residual protection the CAP provides. In those circumstances, no one has any practical idea as to how the farmers might pay their debts. Default on a large scale could bring down the banking sector. There is nothing left in the national exchequer to cushion even the mildest quake in the economy. Colourful talk of a coup by the Irish army is just that: probably enough EEC banks could be strong-armed into a bailing-out exercise. But that of course would mean yet more public debt a frail economy like this has no serious prospect of paying back. Ireland increasingly resembles a study in scarlet.

There are those who whistle to keep their spirits up by arguing that but for the CAP, the situation would be even worse today. Michael Hoey, who runs Ireland's pro-EEC European Movement, lays the blame on successive governments which he accuses of failing to exploit the full advantages of Community membership. Hoey says much of the trouble in agriculture can be blamed on a failure to 'plan for the future'. This must be disingenuous, since the biggest surrender of sovereignty which directly follows a signature to the Treaty of Rome is for each new member to hand over control of agriculture to 800 or so administrators in Brussels. National influence over farming is henceforth redundant. Ireland did enjoy some illusory gains in the early years but, as Professor Sheehy has shown, all have now been wiped out as Brussels wrestles to bring the common agricultural policy under some kind of control. The stark reality that agricultural over-spending threatens to wreck not only the EEC budget but perhaps even the Community itself exercises greater priority in Brussels than the internal afflictions of Ireland. Even Garret 'The Good' Fitzgerald, who confronted deep-rooted shibboleths like divorce, contraception and a unified Irish state, drew the line at challenging the farm lobby. Ireland is always an obstinate force in farming summits: the myth that she has done well out of the CAP for years makes everyone else consider that intransigence as bare-faced cheek.

For fifteen years, only one voice has preached against Ireland's embrace of the EEC. It belongs to Raymond Crotty, a farmer turned academic, who first championed the cause against entry in the 1970s and then went on to throw a massive spanner into the machinery of the Community by single-handedly blocking a far-reaching series of revisions to the Treaty of Rome. Crotty's crusade through the highest courts in Ireland stopped the Dublin government – alone among the twelve – from ratifying treaty changes aimed at overhauling the atrophied decision-making process. He thus succeeded where Lord Denning in Britain, the *Folketing* in Denmark and all ten regional governments in Germany utterly failed. Crotty's detractors dismiss him as a cantankerous eccentric: but the swelling ranks of his admirers prefer the label of remarkable prophet. He has certainly astonished the country by his frankness and a refusal to shrink from disturbing old sensibilities. (The Irish only sourly endorsed the Treaty at a subsequent referendum where the abstention vote was the real winner.)

'Geographically, we are part of Europe but historically and economically, we are part of the Third World,' Crotty tersely declares. 'It was predictable that joining the EEC would prevent us from facing up, as we had already done for 50 years, to what we wanted to do with our independence.' His central thesis is the evolution of Ireland as an outpost of empire. 'The one thing that Ireland shares with all the countries of the undeveloping Third World in the Caribbean, Latin America, Africa and Asia is their colonisation by metropolitan capitalist powers.' Crotty maintains that by joining the EEC, Ireland simply switched from colonial dependence on the British to dependence on Europe as a whole. What he describes as the country's 'tribal pastoralism' and others call the rural economy, has been systematically stripped of value by the common agricultural policy.

In his latest work, *Ireland in Crisis*, Raymond Crotty has ploughed far back into the Celtic past to show the Irish were always on a different path of agricultural evolution, yielding a diet of 'milk and its products, blood drawn from the veins of live animals and meat.' But in neighbouring Britain, people had adopted a mostly crop-based diet by the time of the Norman conquest, quite unsuited to the cold wet climate of Europe's far-westerly offshore island. Then came the potato, an exotic vegetable, which created a coolie class without capital of any kind, condemned to cultivate the land with the meanest tools. Ireland was denied an industrial revolution, and when the potato failed the people starved to death or fled. An emerging Catholic bourgeoisie who were specialists in what Lord Dufferin described as 'all the arts of agitation' led a slow drift to independence. Having acquired self-determination, no one in Ireland knew quite what to do with it. The minor economic boom of the late 1960s and early 1970s looked deceptively like an answer. Irish membership of the EEC would ensure continuing growth, leaving the politicians in the *Dáil* to ponder the attractive problem of distributing the new-found social wealth. Instead of which, as Crotty now astringently puts it, 'we are in a queer old pickle – the debt situation is completely out of control, worse even than Mexico relative to GNP.'

When Charles Haughey returned to power with a razor-blade majority, he railed against those who had run Ireland down as a Third World country, accusing the Irish embassy in London of failing to stop such verbal treason. He conveniently overlooked the fact that most of the critical attention Ireland's economic situation received in the general election came from expatriate Irish journalists who were shocked and disturbed by the fate of their own country. Crotty is in any case unimpressed by what the professional politicians think or do. He is convinced that eventually Ireland's creditors will tire of throwing good money after bad. And then? 'Well, you only have to look at what has happened in the rest of the Third World.'

A guiding principle behind the Treaty of Rome – and the continuous enlargement of the Community to encompass countries like Greece, Portugal, Spain and Ireland, all of whom are wracked by the economic equivalent of the old plague of consumption – is that of transferring resources

153

from the rich to the poor. Raymond Crotty does not say the Irish have been cheated because this has not happened. But the politicians should never have led the people to expect that it would.

11

In England's Green and Pleasant Land

I will not cease from mental fight.
Nor shall my sword sleep in my hand,
Till we have built Jerusalem
In England's green and pleasant land.

William Blake

Thirty years ago, the British people were rudely awakened to something nasty happening in their countryside. The alarm was sounded by Rachel Carson's apocalyptic book, *Silent Spring*, in which she described for the first time, in terms a lay readership might understand, the fearful havoc wrought upon the environment by the chemical agents of over-production. Carson, spiritual founder of the modern ecology movement, warned that the land was being despoiled by fertilisers and pesticides. 'Man,' she reminded her readers, 'is a part of nature. Can he escape a pollution that is now so thoroughly distributed throughout our world?' Her book was an urgent appeal to halt the massive machinery of agriculture and throw it into reverse gear. All that she said went unheeded for a decade and more. In the 1950s, ecology was not only unfashionable: it simply did not exist. The philosophy of plenty, the punishment of soil and pasture to exact more output, at any cost, ruled both government and the food industry. Rachel Carson was dismissed as an eccentric oddity who fretted about the birds and the bees. Thirty years on, we have developed something like six million synthetic chemicals, many of them employed to scrub the land free from pests and weeds which threaten man's crops. Some have compared it to warfare, spray-guns and chemical lances exchanged for rifles and grenades. In consequence there are many places in Britain where the local drinking water is unappetisingly laced with large quantities of nitrates.

The huge chemical industry predictably insists that controls on fertilisers 'will mean higher prices to consumers'. But even the NFU has been forced to concede it would be foolish to ignore the alarm sirens on the use of nitrates which seep from the soil into underground aquifers, rivers, streams and waterways, particularly in the heavily-farmed areas of East Anglia. The long-predicted 'nitrate explosion' is at last with us. There are more than fifty sites in Britain where the nitrate content of drinking water exceeds safety levels prescribed by an EEC directive, which in turn derives from limits proposed by the World Health Organisation. Nitrates are feared because there is medical suspicion of a direct link to stomach cancer and disorders of the liver, spleen and kidneys. The scale of the problem and the major role played by agricultural fertilisers was eventually confirmed by an official report, nervously published at the end of 1986 after prolonged gestation in Whitehall. Its central proposal – the creation of water protection zones in the worst-affected areas – encountered heavy flak from the Ministry of Agriculture. This nicely illustrates the new 'green gap' in British politics, because the Department of the Environment strongly favours protection zones where fertiliser dosage could be stringently controlled. The question of who should compensate farmers not to use fertilisers soon arose, the NFU bleating that farmers' sons should not be punished for what their fathers had done at the behest of governments who constantly urged them on to produce more and cheaper food.

The Danes are now thoroughly alarmed at the nitrate

threat -- confirmed by massive deoxygenation of shallow coastal waters and devastation of aquatic life including fish stocks. The government in Copenhagen is under pressure to impose a mandatory reduction of at least 25% in the use of all nitrate-based fertilisers. But there and in every other EEC country, the farm lobby is fighting a rearguard action against nitrate controls. An official report in Holland mournfully concluded that 'simply restricting nitrate inputs would lead to a very marked reduction in farming income'. At the same time, the Dutch are wrestling with the malodorous consequences of a mountain of dung produced by the country's five million cows and 12 million pigs. This alpine accumulation of animal waste – nearly 100 million tonnes every year – is the source of much black comedy. The harassed Dutch call it their 'spreading problem' because there is literally nowhere left in such a small country to spray or dump it safely. This excessively strong cocktail of harmful chemicals like nitrates and phosphates poses a severe environmental threat to rivers, lakes and canals. They even tried the bizarre concept of 'dung banks' where farmers could unload surplus excrement, but now those are overflowing too.

As a by-product of the CAP, the Dutch manure mountain has naturally acquired all the characteristics of a growth industry. Simply storing it costs 2 billion guilders a year. Carting the stuff around to manure-deficient areas has spawned a small but prosperous specialised transport industry. But since much of the waste is so toxic, the government has been compelled on scientific advice to bring in new laws which control the expansion of piggeries and poultry units. Farmers will also be fined if they exceed permited levels of dung output, and soil-protection limits are being imposed. And finally a new national 'manure bank' is being established to make the best use of what the Dutch agricultural ministry, with considerable imagination, describes as a 'national resource'. Maybe so, but

Holland's neighbours in the EEC have nevertheless turned up their noses at it, sending clear warning signals that truckloads of phosphate-enriched dung trundling over the frontiers will not be welcomed.

Even when farm ministers are told by their own scientific advisers that the quantity of chemicals dumped on the land can be drastically reduced without damaging the quality or yield of crops, the advice is invariably pigeon-holed. Work done at the Ministry of Agriculture's own private research farm at Bloxworth in Cambridgeshire falls precisely into that category. A report in May 1986 which gives a virtual clean sheet to environmentally-friendly farming practices has been effectively suppressed, on the political grounds that it might provoke an uncomfortable public row about farmers' costs and subsidies and reveal the true scale of chemical pollution in the countryside. The Ministry clings to the idea that farmers can be weaned towards the 'rational use' of chemicals by a patient process of education. The same philosophy is echoed in France and Germany. Reckoning up the acres of page-space bought by fertiliser companies every week in the glossy farming weeklies, this looks a forlorn hope. The chemical industry can have no vested interest in reducing consumption or, for that matter, production.

Britain has some 30 million acres of good farmland. The constantly upward spiral of increasing yield would, by itself, render at least a quarter of that largely superfluous by the year 2000. This is primarily due to the quickening rate of technical advance, the 'technology bypass' which the CAP's creator, Sicco Mansholt, entirely overlooked 30 years ago and continues to discount today. If all the politicians in the country closed the barn doors and went home, it would take at least 50 years and probably more to correct the havoc wrought by total farming. About a third of the country's landscape has suffered the worst degradation from excessive exploitation. A report to the European Parliament in autumn 1986 suggested that soil erosion in the most intensively farmed areas of Britain was reaching alarming proportions, in Greece had blighted a quarter of the land under cultivation and in southern France actually threatened desertification of previously highly-fertile territory. Another survey shows that erosion in the Bedfordshire wheatlands between 1973 and 1979 was twenty times above acceptable tolerance levels.

Soil is not something to be taken for granted, a gift of nature which will handily renew itself despite the predations of man. Even in ideal conditions, good soil takes between 200 and 400 years to form. It is part of a complex matrix weaving together underground water sources, essential vegetation like tree and plant life and the natural influence of the climate. The European Parliament report threw the blame for the emerging dust-bowl syndrome squarely at heavy agriculture encouraged by the CAP, urging the immediate arrest of the most damaging soil-bruising activities and a massive tree-planting programme to expand the moisture reservoir. If our grandchildren were not to find themselves living in a desert, a huge redirection of resources was essential to switch the funds spent on storing unwanted food surpluses into a concerted plan of repair for exhausted, overworked land.

Yet British people – by which I mean those who live and work in an urban environment – persist in regarding the rurality of all they see around them as a fantasia, timeless, unchanging and only recently bruised by farming practices. In truth what they see is essentially the legacy of the last great agricultural revolution, the sweeping process of enclosure which commenced in the late Middle Ages and reached a legislative peak in the years from 1773 to 1868. The Earl of Clarendon wrote ecstatically of how the writ of parliament would take a land 'encumbered with bushes and briars, like a deformed forest . . . to be cultivated and polished'. Two thousand separate enclosure acts swept away ancient heath and common land alike. The experience of one small community in the 1850s was sadly instructive. Six hundred villagers who had subsisted on a 300-acre common woke up to find it enclosed by a dozen stave-armed landlords: the yeomen were left with five-acre allotments to keep starvation from their doors. The small cottage industries which maintained the soul of rural England – brick-making, charcoal-burning, wood-cutting, brewing – gave up the sap of life. Some contemporary observers wrote about enclosure as a moral tragedy: but precipitators like Clarendon considered that bigger and better farms were essential to feed the industrial masses. Not only the landscape changed utterly. Enclosure enfranchised and expanded farmer control of the Tory Party, until Disraeli invented 'villa conservatism' to challenge it. The Reform Acts of 1832 and 1867 reversed the anachronistic domination of the rural vote, extending suffrage to town and city dwellers: yet the rural grip on the British political conscience has never been entirely released, which is why agriculture still has a minister of its own, with a seat at the Cabinet table.

Enclosure erased whole villages, destroying an emerging rural proletariat which then underwent deportation into the compressed and teeming stews of industrial Victorian Britain. A century on, that legacy abides with us today, as the debilitated remnants of great conurbations creak and groan now the industrial tide is sweeping out again in a new direction.

Those squalls of change are also whipping fiercely through the countryside again, just as they did in the days of the enclosure acts. For the first time, the supremacy of the common agricultural policy (and its closely-related cousins elsewhere) is being seriously challenged. There is an emerging consensus favouring change as necessary and inevitable. Defining the extent of that consensus, and the practical reality of what can be done, is much more difficult. Farmers are worried and unsettled, strapped down by artificial production controls and at the same time addicted to public subsidy and private debt. National opinion is increasingly insensitive, sustaining the distorted image of an industry on the fast track of subsidised generosity.

It is true that the common agricultural policy has created a new breed of agri-millionaires. But as Professor Colin Spedding argues, that lens has warped the picture. Wealthy farmers who own their land and avoided borrowing have done particularly well out of CAP incentives: the gradual slide in land prices we are now experiencing is simply a paper devaluation for such lucky ones. The indebted farmer – especially a tenant with limited security – is faced with few alternatives. 'What we actually have,' says Spedding, 'is a surplus of young, technically-minded, modern farmers who took advantage of opportunities to borrow money and invest and are now caught in a trap. The odds point strongly to the proposition that if we are going to get control of surpluses, then this is going to mean shock horror for a considerable proportion of indebted farmers.' This will mean gloomy tidings for the High Street banks, who have underwritten to the tune of millions practically every small farmer in the country. In so doing, they have institutionalised a regime based on subsistence income which would collapse without the nourishment of public subsidy. It is a money-go-round of debt feeding debt. Would anyone have done that in the commercial world outside agriculture where such lavish insulation is not so easily available?

The tolerance limits of small farming enterprises are highly susceptible to even modest changes in policy. Spedding's 'shock horror' scenario seems grimly inevitable from an analysis of economic returns taken on the fringe of farming Britain. A man with 60 acres to keep 80 or so cows, plus say 20 for corn, a shade more again to grow cereals and ten devoted to oilseeds – presents an example of highly-exposed risk. After rounding up all the available subsidies and earning a premium on milking (the EEC price for milk is roughly £100 per cow above world prices), our man is left with a paper-thin 'profit' of about £7,500 after meeting all the input costs such as feed, fuel, seeds, farmhouse overheads and wages. This is not the stuff of fortune-building. Knock out the CAP support and the notional profit evaporates. Expansion is limited by quota regimes imposed by Brussels (and potential evacuation from the national warchest of subsidies.)

These are Britain's social farmers, whose incomes are sustained for reasons which are only distantly related to a managed food policy. The tragic fact is that small farmers working marginal land are strategically unnecessary and may shortly be fully expendable. The EEC has tacitly recognised this by introducing incentive schemes to en-courage retirement, which of course is a cypher for mergers and the agglomeration of larger units which are insured by their greater viability against major shifts in policy. In manufacturing industry, this process of rationalisation is a commonplace reaction to adjustments in marketing climates. With the CAP, social engineers tried to armour-plate a large part of agriculture against all exterior in-fluences. The result is a very few wealthy entrepreneurs and many more living on borrowed time and money.

The process of farm mergers derived new energy from milk quotas, which are now tradeable as a form of invisible currency, although no one has yet defined substantively whether they are legal tender if the Brussels remit is strictly applied. As quotas bit into farming incomes, it soon became attractive to shift milk about the country with paper transfers. Those leaving the industry get an attractive fillip for their retirement if they can sell their quota to someone else who wants to stay in business but needs more milk output to survive. Taken to its logical conclusion, a handful of dairy farmers bent on dominating the industry could eventually buy up the right to produce all the milk in the country, creating one vast mega-dairy. The troglodytes running the 'central committee' in Brussels have still not explained how the CAP can lay any claim to social credentials if its only net effect is to make it impossible for small farmers to stay on the land.

The industry is therefore beset by Valkyries on all sides. The first, provocative gestures made by the British government towards a long-term evolution in policy are a reflex reaction to the uncertainties created in turn by the EEC. The urban-dwelling majority, deeply disenchanted with the CAP because of antics like taxing consumers in order to sell cheap butter to the Russians, are nevertheless perturbed when 'their' countryside seems to be a candidate for un-settling change. Uproar therefore followed the first tenta-tive steps towards a new policy which would replace the previous obsession with production at any price. This can only mean redundancy for farmers and farmland alike, but ministers who tinker with the Green Belt or threaten to let the developers loose in national parks are certain to court public rage. And that is precisely what erupted when Whitehall got its wires crossed early in 1987 on the presentation of a radical policy change in rural land management.

For the best part of two years, a special joint committee linking two powerful rival ministries (environment and agriculture) worked in bunker-like secrecy to perfect a grand new scenario, code-named appealingly ALURE – alternative land use for the rural economy. It is widely accepted that Environment, which has been itching for years to get its fingers into much of the Ministry of Agriculture pie, had the whip-hand in Alure's international policy design. Nicholas Ridley, Mrs Thatcher's 'dry but not brittle' implant at Environment, was soon cast as the Jack Horner of the piece. Ridley, who has no love for the CAP, had been eagerly awaiting his chance drastically to reshape Britain's cumbrous system of land-use controls. It is now plain that much of the national reserve of farming land will be coming out of direct production – even if the CAP were left just to lumber on over the cliff. The question the Alure team had to answer was how to control the retreat from total farming in such a way that it did not become a rout before an army of unscrupulous developers.

Ridley was capably backed up by his departmental minister for environmental matters, William Waldegrave, whose father is a major landowner in Somerset's Mendip country. Waldegrave is shot through with Prince Charles-like anxieties about the impact of total farming and a practician of change at the same time. He and Ridley represent a complete contrast to Michael Jopling at Agriculture, who would like nothing better than the status quo, if only it were not for the monstrous problems imposed by over-production. Jopling, detecting vibes of radicalism intruding into his own patch, moved several times to nail up no-poaching signs. But he was effectively restrained by the plotting on Alure, although its blanket of secrecy was already developing moth-holes.

Early in 1987 the media picked up signals that Mrs Thatcher was about to do a U-turn on the farming lobby. Once the work had been compromised by leaks, it was essential to lift at least a corner in order to forestall a shock reaction amongst the farming community. Or so the Ministry of Agriculture thought, utterly failing to appreciate that the real backlash would come from the towns and not the country vote. The press turned out to be right. Alure is a vintage example of placing a land-mine under a sour old problem. Unfortunately, premature explosion almost blew apart much of the emerging consensus on a new role for rural Britain and also detonated a spate of trench warfare between the two rival ministries. Whatever is said now as an exercise in damage-limitation cannot conceal a deep split in Whitehall which places the survival of the Ministry of Agriculture itself at risk.

In February 1987 Michael Jopling was facing acute discomfort as the NFU manœuvred against the stringent cuts in beef and milk support schemes won at the Battle of Brussels on 16 December the previous year. Drawing every ounce of strength from its weakening muscles, the union proclaimed that it was 'after Jopling's blood'. To draw the fire away from his embattled ministry, Jopling hurried off to the NFU annual meeting at Kensington Town Hall and let the Alure cat (or kitten, since at the time of writing, it has still not reached full maturity) out of the bag. The *Daily Telegraph* tartly observed that he had made a 'belated attempt to capture the high ground in the environmental debate', but in so doing achieved the considerable feat of uniting farmers and environmentalists in dissatisfaction against him. The Whitehall village was even less circumspect, complaining that Jopling had botched up the presentation of long overdue reforms, allowing half-informed detractors to run away with a picture of England as a land 'fit only for bungalows and conifers'. In the lobby, Ridley's men accused the Minister of Agriculture of trampling all over their sensitive plans 'with his great size twelve green wellies'. Responding to a back-bench questioner in the Commons, Mrs Thatcher fixed a withering eye on the two front-bench miscreants and coldly agreed that it would be a good idea if in future the two Ministries got their act together by issuing joint statements. Ridley was infuriated because the opposition parties tore into his careful work as a licence for urban sprawl and the downhill march of yet more gloomy fir plantations. Trapped in the cross-fire and shot at from all sides, Michael Jopling's credibility rating plummeted to zero. Only a few weeks before he had returned from Brussels like Alexander. Party mandarins stirred uneasily at the tumult, which provoked disturbing pre-election tensions in potentially important rural seats.

As to Alure itself, while Ridley's team had tried to work out how to stop developers swarming over acres of redundant farmland, the Ministry of Agriculture had the task of decking out the store with attractive alternative lures for the farmers themselves. They came up with a snack rather than a feast, about £25 million of strictly-tailored incentives, from more subsidies to expand forestry to extra help to relieve pressure on 'environmentally sensitive areas' like the Norfolk Broads and the Somerset wetlands. At Kensington one delegate likened the package to a 'spit in the ocean' compared to the arithmetic of the CAP.

Meanwhile, the effective lord of the landscape, Nicholas Ridley, pushed on with the real business in hand, and the meat of Alure, his ministry's draft circular on redeploying the agricultural land which now seemed likely to go out of intensive production. Ridley is composed of politically fissionable material, commanding one of the largest interventionist departments of state whilst by taste and inspiration a high priest of the market. His impatience with subsidy and what he calls 'state mummery' naturally places him at odds with an unreconstructed traditional agrarian like Michael Jopling. Ridley is more of a sophisticate than many think – he writes and paints well, and loves gardening. His wit is acerbic and often gets him into trouble. As an engineer by trade, he likes to introduce the bulldozer to intractable problems. Jopling, who consummated a lifetime's ambition when he moved from the chief whip's chambers to agriculture, was shell-shocked for days by his treatment at the hands of the NFU. He is unencumbered with intellectual baggage and sees himself as a farmer up in town. Once it became unavoidable to postpone any longer a programme of radical change in the countryside, Ridley and Jopling were bound to collide head on. And, as events dictated, Ridley was to survive as Jopling stumbled and fell.

When the clouds of dust settled the government made a fresh attempt at lifting the wraps from Alure. No less than five ministries – environment, agriculture and the three dependencies in Wales, Scotland and Ulster – brought out *Farming and Rural Enterprise* in brotherly harmony in March 1987. The document exuded the distinctive tone of Nicholas Ridley, echoing the new mood in Westminster and Whitehall. Nothing was held back about the follies of the CAP, such as the dramatic expansion in cereal production which had turned Britain into a major exporter for the first time. Now we can bury Malthus, we are told, since 'the explosion in technology has overtaken the growth in population'. And, tracing a link directly back to the work of Sicco Mansholt and his friends, one highly significant sentence was picked out in black: 'The government continues to believe that the root cause of imbalance between supply and demand is that prices are set too high.' Amen to that, consumers will say, but the plain truth is that the British government alone cannot arrest the CAP juggernaut, because just like the farmers, the governments of the European Community are caught in the subsidy trap. To make any impression on output, price cuts must be draconian to stop food being sucked into the intervention stores. Drastic cuts will leave farmers at the apex of the great pyramid of subsidies unscathed. They can survive a regime which deflates EEC food production levels and influences the emergence of a new global average. But the small farmers will be put out of business in their thousands. And that makes nonsense of the holy ethos of self-sufficiency which has prevailed since the CAP was born, not to mention the social pretentions of the agricultural policy.

Artificial intrusions like quotas – as Professor David Grigg of Sheffield University argues – serve only to fossilise an industry. That is exactly what has happened to the European steel industry since it came under the direct mandate of Brussels during 'a state of manifest crisis'. Whether it be quotas or cuts makes little difference to the small farmer about to be shown the door by the evolution of policy change in Brussels and Whitehall. The British government's candid decision to confront the food crisis on the home front is still far ahead of any initiative mounted in Brussels or anywhere else in the EEC. But of itself, it is bound to be a diversionary action rather than a frontal attack, since to strike through into the open ground it is necessary either to abolish the common agricultural policy or to unhitch individual countries and let them go their own way. And there is a further risk attached to weaning farmers from one set of subsidies only to hook them almost immediately on another medicine chest of tranquillisers.

Peter Pooley in Brussels castigates the notion of turning food producers into 'grockle farmers', harvesting the rents from seaside caravans and country chalets instead of beef and barley. 'Quite simply, we have to be careful they don't want paying for that as well.' First experience with selective opt-out payments to farmers to mind how they go in environmentally-sensitive areas is not encouraging. There has been plenty of loud talk about grants 'we can't wipe our faces with'. Greed might play a part in that, but the reality is that farmers who are tending land in areas of natural beauty are the ones under most pressure to spare the plough and the nitrates. And they are also the ones who have never shared in the profits creamed from the great cereals explosion, for example. A small lowland farm – typical, say, of the Welsh valleys or the Scottish borders – running 60 beef cattle and 250 ewes with a small cereal acreage – collects nearly £9,000 a year in subsidies. And after deduction of all on-farm costs, that represents an astonishing 307% of net income. It will require a heavy dosage of environmental tranquillisers to allow farmers working with balance sheets of that sort to sleep easily at night. Equally, the employment of subsidies is always a mockery of natural economic laws: to justify such largesse on the grounds that small farmers are wardens of the landscape is to invert the government's brave decision to face out the miners when they demanded an open public purse to defend impoverished communities caught in the cycle of industrial change.

The Conservatives have already confessed – in William Waldegrave's words – that the countryside is no longer a factory for food. This sounds theoretically earth-moving. But is it so? The wild land of Britain was cleaner, more attractive and less polluted before the great dig for victory, let alone the CAP. Now that ministers have discovered trees (as the writer Simon Jenkins says, ideology flies out of the window when electoral interest enters the door), it seems that Birnam wood will play another important part on the stage of history. A bright button in Whitehall has decided that our balance of payments in timber is worm-eaten, that we import too much. If we pay farmers to crop trees – especially the ecologically-seductive ones, like oaks and elms – 'we will be better off'. That is the old deceptive lure of self-sufficiency, and the result will be another forest of subsidies which some future distracted government will be forced to chop down.

Farmers are compelled to observe the emerging drama with hypnotic fascination. Decisions which affect their livelihood are taken every day with little reference to their views. The marriage of farmland to government is a contract which ensures that the industry has lost the power of independent decision. 'If you sup with the devil, you should use a long spoon,' is a warning that farmers ignored when they surrendered private initiative in favour of public subsidy. Since 1979, support for the energy industry has turned around completely from a £550 million deficit to a projected surplus of about the same amount in 1988. Industrial subsidies have been chopped in half, from £2.4 billion, over the same period. Yet agriculture – economically and politically insignificant – was hoisted from £830 million to £2.2 billion in 1987; and is still rising. Sir Richard Body has argued powerfully what might have been done with that money if it had been injected as mortar into the battlements of new technology. Not a single job has been preserved – pickled would be a better word – by this torrent of singular generosity. The proposition that paying farmers to do nothing, or much less of what they do already, is about as cost-effective as the promotion of fish-farming in the Serpentine.

12

A Song Without End

Oh the buzzing of the bees
In the cigarette trees,
The soda water fountain,
Where the lemonade springs
And the bluebird sings
On that big rock candy mountain.

traditional American folk song

The thirtieth anniversary of the Treaty of Rome on 25 March 1987 was a suitably joyless occasion. In Brussels it was just another working day. Plans for the European Parliament to migrate to Italy for a splendid birthday feast were thankfully aborted. In truth there was little to celebrate. A bankrupt Community some £17 billion adrift downstairs in the accounts department could hardly afford to send out for a crate of champagne. No presents were exchanged. The anniversary itself was marked only by a characteristically sour impasse over plans to set up a big-spending project devoted to research in high-technology. Where, British and German ministers queried, would the money come from? Only days before, the European Commission sent an unusually terse and succinct communication to Parliament, describing why the EEC was in Carey Street: 'The Community has sunk into a morass of budgetary mal-practices . . . the unprecedented build-up of agricultural stocks has been disguised by gross over-valuation . . . Community commitments have been allowed to accumulate without proper financial provisions.' In other words, as Peter Price has said, people who allow that sort of chaos to prevail over their affairs should be certified. This stricture must include Jacques Delors, president of the European Commission, who is in a weak position to issue homilies on improvidence. The gaggle of mediocrities over whom he presides – the majority of them failed refugees from frustrated political careers at home – are hardly noted for team spirit or their dedication to the EEC. The seventeen commissioners are all supposed to renounce national loyalty once installed in Brussels, taking a solemn oath never to serve any other master. In practice, the strings to which they are attached lead straight back to their own national capitals. Delors himself has been caught out more than once talking about French rather than Community interest at gatherings for the Brussels press corps. The Commission is riven by factional in-fighting which frequently degenerates into the kind of chauvinistic squabbling which Delors thinks is responsible for the financial ruin of the Community. Viewed in that light, the Commission's majestic sermon on the impecunious state of the EEC's finances is drained of meaning.

While the bickering continues, the ship of state drifts closer to the rocks. The last time the EEC was faced with a seemingly insurmountable financial crisis, member states had their arms twisted to hand over more cash. They agreed to a change in the financial regulations which govern how much each country contributes. They are less than keen to agree to a repeat performance because the new budget arrangements, intended to last three years, did not allow for the blotting paper of the CAP. It took just nine months to run out of ready cash once again. The *apparatchiks* in Brussels have refused to accept any of the blame, arguing only that the member states refused to heed their danger signals on the burgeoning growth of farm expenditure. In standard Brussels jargon, this means a 'shortfall in resources' for which more money is the only known cure. The CAP may have bankrupted the Community but everything in the garden would be lovely if member states released the EEC budget from an impossibly short leash and allowed it to expand in direct proportion to the demands made upon it. This is a recipe for infinite expansion of the farm policy. And lest anyone should be in doubt, farm commissioner Frans Andriessen told a special committee of Euro MPs probing food surpluses that 'self-sufficiency in European agriculture could not be called into question'. Which makes one wonder whether the journey of so many EEC officials to negotiate with their American opposite numbers at Geneva is really necessary.

The Commission cannot even find a target card for anyone to aim at. Pressed by MEPs to suggest what a basic strategic minimum might be for stocks of basic foodstuffs, the response is always that no one can be precisely sure. Because food production in Europe has soared out of control, governments have been deluded into thinking that they have created genuine export markets. But dumping EEC food merely displaces the huge excesses which already exist on the world market. 'Geldof's garden', the Third World, suffers worst from this selfish folly: but the longer it continues, the more likely it will be that the Americans will tire of trading insults with the Europeans and move on to punitive sanctions in the political arena.

Only the enormous food deficiency of the Soviet Union has so far deflected the coming crisis. Now analysts have begun to detect significant changes in Soviet husbandry which could take the Russians off the world food market as a major purchasing power by the end of this century. The 1986 Soviet grain harvest was the best on record and barring some unexpected reverse (a third of Russia's winter grain crop was for instance seriously affected by severe frosts in 1987) it is likely that the days of bumper American and EEC grain sales behind the Iron Curtain are over. One western expert believes the Russians will cross the 250-million-tonne barrier inside five years, which if true contains a chilling message for the CAP, since at that point Russia will not only reach self-sufficiency but begin to acquire the capability to export.

This quantum leap in the Russian food situation has been achieved mainly by changes in technique and improvements to transport so that less of the crop is wasted by bureaucratic muddling. But Gorbachev's 'new deal' with its strong emphasis on productivity is certain to work a further transformation. Milk and butter production is already being shaken up to eliminate serious wastage: but output has in any case risen modestly for several years. And not all of Soviet agriculture is an automatic disaster area. Thanks to extensive irrigation and introduction of new technology, the Russians are the world's third biggest cotton fibre producer and the second largest exporter. It is a private nightmare inside the European Commission that Communist agriculture is on the road to self-sufficiency: if it reaches a genuine exportable status, then world food production will reach over-kill. Even the vestigial 'export' markets which exist today will disappear. What happened in Saudi Arabia is a telling pointer. The dusty desert kingdom spent an oil fortune irrigating the desert, and the green revolution which followed has given the country an exportable wheat surplus of some 1.7 million tonnes a year.

There is a direct link between the tragedy of the CAP and the continued decline in Europe's share of the world industrial cake. We already know that the Japanese have made off with the icing. Within the next decade, she will replace the USA in second place in the league table, while the EEC will stick at number three position and continue to stagnate. Since 1957, the Community has managed to win only a tiny extra portion – and that is only achieved by throwing in a few crumbs of creative accountancy on trade between the various members of a gradually-enlarging community. Europe's research and development spending, the lifeblood of the future, makes similarly depressing reading. The Japanese are the big spenders on R & D, almost 3% of their gross domestic product, a nose ahead of the Americans. The total EEC figure is a pathetic 1.8%.

Because spending on agriculture looks so low as a percentage of total GDP in Europe, apologists for the CAP argue that taxpayers should eat up their ample supplies of good quality food and stop carping. Turn the argument the other way around and it does not look so appealing. The CAP entirely distorts the EEC budget, swallowing nearly two-thirds of it just to maintain a minority industry at a grossly-inflated standard of living. Even to maintain the EEC at the 1987 level of activity will require a hike of around 50% over the next five years, which is far more than any of the member states are prepared to contemplate.

That is why the 'big three' – Germany, France and the United Kingdom – spent the EEC's thirtieth birthday quibbling over the sums for a trivial proposal to put some pace back into the high-technology race with Japan and the United States. Its cost, in budgetary terms, is negligible: but the bitter truth is that because of the appetite of the CAP, there is no cash to pay for it. And while the French and Germans in particular will always fight to the last ear of corn to maintain the sanctity of the farm policy, the equal irony is that they have no intention of letting the EEC set up in business with yet more mismanaged and ill-conceived projects containing a built-in propensity to acquire a life of their own. So the real seed corn – research and development – is allowed to wither and die.

At thirty years old, the European Community is a victim of premature middle age, haunted by the indiscretions of youth and unable to shake off bad habits. What is clearly required is a sense of dedication to make a new start. The biggest test of whether it can will be the ultimate outcome of the attempts to inject some sense of financial propriety into the management of the CAP. Future, if not present, governments might then be prepared to view with favour a community which allocates its spending priorities wisely. Fewer people than ever now expect to see an integrated federation of European states in their own lifetime. That is a measure of the dream which has failed. By the time we create a genuine internal common market – if we ever do – the EEC will be just short of its fortieth birthday. The erosion of Europe's share of world trade continues unabated. Instead of widening and deepening a sense of community with friendly allied powers like the United States, the Europeans are locked in fratricidal conflicts. The door to the east is on the latch, but development of a pan-European political consensus on how to treat with the Soviet Union is confused by distracting internal rows over the mess in the farmyard and the contents of the cash-register. The Third World is being progressively stripped of the opportunity to stimulate its own growth – and thus achieve a degree of economic dignity and independence – by the EEC's restrictions on food imports. Europe remains a political and economical dwarf on the world stage, stunted by an unnatural obsession with agriculture. Historians will find this very odd.

There is an alternative. It requires an ideological sea-change in attitudes, but given the gradual erosion of socialism and the late 20th-century reversion to fundamentalism in the market-place, Europe can yet escape from the self-imposed fetters of the CAP. The Community must gradually but progressively evacuate from all farm support structures. Critics deride the free-market vision of agriculture as a mirage, but on closer examination it appears to possess remarkable qualities of substance. For a start, the pressure to produce for its own sake vanishes the moment the cash is no longer available. Land-bruisers will be compelled to spare the plough and the insecticide once the bottomless resource of incentive disappears. The enormous shift towards intensive culture – and thus, ever-larger farming units – would undergo a degree of correction, although this assertion should not be pushed too far since agglomeration pursued for genuine efficiency is as valid in agriculture as in any other industry. But far more small to medium-sized farmers would survive and flourish once bureaucracy was removed from their backs. This is because many would revert to enterprises in scale and harmony with the local environment.

Farm shops and pick-your-own crop initiatives continue to multiply by a factor of about ten per cent in Britain every year. Many are now becoming sophisticated operations, selling off-farm produce as well as high quality food like vegetables, fruit, meat, cheese, cream and other dairy products. It would prove possible to re-invent the English tomato, as well as restoring much else of the traditional flavour of English country life. By abolishing the heinous monopoly of the Milk Marketing Board, the government could, at a stroke, deliver a new lease of life to languishing doorstep delivery rounds, particularly by encouraging those which already specialise in the added value of distributing other kinds of fresh food door-to-door. Too many farmers in Britain are foolishly nervous about combining into producing, retailing and wholesaling co--operatives. This beggar-my-neighbour attitude of self-destruction remains a powerful force. But once the fresh breezes of competition were to blow through the industry, they would be left with little choice.

The Cheddar Valley in Somerset, which once fed daily special trains speeding strawberries to market in Birmingham and London, is a case in point. The local horticultural industry, mostly fragmented and disorganised, has had a tough time at the hands of efficiency-disposed foreign competitors. The horticultural industry's failure to shift itself out of decades of indolence and mutual suspicion has handed an entire market on a plate to the Dutch, Italians, and even the *kibbutzim* of the Negev. 'Alternative land use' can mean the development of multi-crop farms which blur the old boundaries between horticulture and agriculture: farmers will be left to themselves to judge what to grow for the market, and at what price. By getting together in co-operative units, they can spread the high cost inputs of mechanisation and labour, and even target themselves to service major outlets like supermarkets – which are increasingly geared to volume suppliers like the Dutch because no one in Britain can be bothered to compete. In an age which is becoming quality- instead of quantity-conscious, there is a vast untapped market for ready-to-eat food straight out of the countryside. Britain's farmers could lead the fight against the dreary, bland texture of sameness which afflicts the national diet. Of course many farmers who do not relish a liberalised industry free from subsidy will simply sell up and get off the land. And for the first time in generations, young people, eager and willing to work, will find a farm waiting for them, at a price they can afford.

The development of recreation in the countryside – a trenchant theme running through the thinking of the Alure team – stands to gain an enormous boost in an agricultural economy unhitched from the bogeymen in Whitehall and Brussels. Peter Pooley's 'grockle parks' – serried ranks of caravans spilling down to the cliff edge – are too often the direct result of the desperate need for a cash harvest to feed the overdraft. But there is nothing intrinsically wrong with the development of farm holidays, based on economical units tailored to the environment: the ones which will really succeed are those where entrepreneurs offer extra value – horse-riding, fishing lessons, country craft and wisdom, hiking, even a chance to help out with the milking and the cheese-making. As H. G. Wells used to say, 'Why not, why not?'

What we can be absolutely sure of is that the continuance of the CAP will turn the traditional small farmer into a vanishing species. That will be true in Britain, France, Bavaria, or anywhere else in the Common Market. But a free market in olive oil, for example, would not only retain and secure a traditional rural base in Italy and Spain but inspire the price of olive oil itself to drop like a stone down into the everyday consumption zone: at that point, the Mafia would pick on another activity to exploit and release their poisonous grip on the EEC budget.

The invigorating zest of market forces implies a return to the world free market. On the one hand, that restrains the compulsion to weld grain-producing land into one vast prairie: on the other, it offers the consumer the automatic balancing act required to hold the major food commodities at around the prevailing world price level. Most farmers, and some economists, argue that the result of the EEC, or even of Britain alone, returning to major purchasing on the world market would be a major upward trend in prices. In the case of sugar, to give a key example, that would certainly be inevitable, because the depressive effect of over-production would be suddenly switched into reverse. But since EEC sugar production is subsidised so recklessly, the difference to consumers would prove marginal. Cereal prices would, in general, decline: dairy products – particularly milk and butter – would fall impressively at first, and then recover, but still end up floating well below today's inflated prices. The long-suffering dairy producers, if only they would open their eyes, have most to gain from an unregulated market which can serve attractive and expanding local economies, as well as supplying national outlets through the major dairy-processing firms.

Is it possible, at least within the context of the EEC? Britain's participation in the CAP is an obligation not easily discarded, a major stumbling block to any independent reform of agriculture outside a Community consensus.

Clearly the most attractive answer is to put the axe to the entire world food subsidy system at the GATT talks in Geneva, but there are few who will argue optimistically for rapid progress there, despite the optimistic melodies hummed at the Venice economic summit. A world trade war – the EEC picking up sides against the USA and Japan – might serve to concentrate minds. Alternatively, the principal member states of the Community might privately conspire to permit the CAP to expire quietly: even in Brussels, there are some patient advocates of that approach. Or the British could imperceptibly disengage from the more impossible appurtenances of the CAP – a thought to send shivers down every spine in the Foreign Office. They may not know a cow from a calf but playing rough with the CAP always ends up with Britain's *communautaire* credentials being dragged through the dirt yet again.

One is left with the force of dogged argument, trying to persuade everyone else in the club to see it our way. The Alure process could be seen as a constructive element in a long end-game, except that as Professor Colin Spedding argues, insufficient thought is being devoted to practical alternatives to the CAP. The principle of subsidy has permeated the system so deeply that no one seems willing to think sensibly about a world of agriculture which does without it. The accumulating afflictions of the CAP do present a window of opportunity: the British, at least, seem willing to open it a notch or two and sniff the fresh air outside. Some people detect a faint desire among the French and Germans to unlock the casements and ponder the view. This appears to represent heresy, the so-called 're-nationalisation of agriculture' by each of the twelve member states. And that is enough to send the inquisition in the Palais d'Berlaymont reaching for the thumb-screws.

The awful reality is that Europe is spinning down the road to irrelevance. Agriculture, since the 1950s, has never really been a suitable issue to obsess an emerging European political confederation. If genuine monetary union had been achieved fifteen or twenty years ago, most of the CAP's undesirable limbs might have been hacked off and burned by now. Perhaps. The road to reform, if anyone is willing to take it, must somehow surmount the formidable barrier imposed by Mansholt's promise, set in concrete, to maintain the incomes of farmers, whatever the cost. Until subsidy in farming is ripped out by its roots, Europe can never truly flower.

APPENDIX I

The 1985 EEC Budget

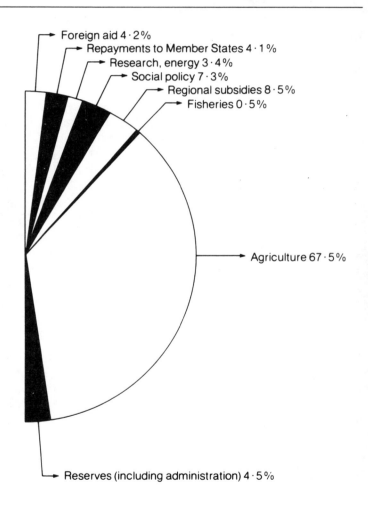

Foreign aid 4·2%
Repayments to Member States 4·1%
Research, energy 3·4%
Social policy 7·3%
Regional subsidies 8·5%
Fisheries 0·5%

Agriculture 67·5%

Reserves (including administration) 4·5%

APPENDIX II

The Institutions of the EEC

Administration of the European Community is slow, cumbersome and, many will argue, ineffective, because of the lack of any self-willed power structure. The core of the Community is represented by the EUROPEAN COMMISSION, the civil service based in Brussels which displays powerful political pretentions. This is because the body is charged with collegiate responsibility to protect the TREATY OF ROME (creating the European Economic Community, signed Rome, 25 March 1956). Seventeen Commissioners (including a president – present incumbent Jacques Delors, from France) are appointed to serve four-year terms. Larger countries including Britain are allowed two Commissioners, the minnows one. No woman has yet been appointed.

The Commission proposes Community legislation, in the first instance to the EUROPEAN PARLIAMENT, which since 1979 has been directly elected. The Parliament suffers from its restricted consultative role, although it does have important powers in budgetary affairs and can effectively delay the legislative process by imaginative exploitation of its rules of procedure. Parliament's powers will be enhanced under the Treaty changes known as the SINGLE EUROPEAN ACT aimed at modernising the Community's decision-making process, but a constitutional crisis in Ireland – provoked by Mr Raymond Crotty – delayed implementation.

All legislation must pass the COUNCIL OF MINISTERS,

the body visualised by the founding fathers as the government of the Community. In practice, it has fallen miserably short of that status. There is no single Council – each one is specifically composed of ministers from member state governments to deal with a specific issue, such as agriculture.

The EUROPEAN COUNCIL represents the Crown Jewels – the heads of state gathered in conclave. In fact, this body is a recent creation and was never foreseen in the Treaty.

The COURT OF JUSTICE (not to be confused with the entirely unrelated Court of Human Rights at Strasbourg) exists to resolve disputes between Community institutions and member states and is the final arbiter of the Treaty and Community legislation: but it has no enforcement powers.

The COURT OF AUDITORS is charged with the responsibility of going over the books.

Some terms:

GATT: General Agreement on Tariffs and Trade. The post-war-world regulating body charged with management of trade between its consenting parties (effectively, the Western democracies and their acolytes).

EEC: The European Economic Community, which, when known as the EC (European Communities), combines Euratom and the European Coal and Steel Community.

EMS: The European Monetary System. Foreseen as a major step to economic and monetary union between the member states. Britain is not a full member (she commits a portion of sterling to EMS reserves but does not participate in the exchange mechanism) and Greece, Spain and Portugal have not so far joined either. The EMS maintains participating currencies within an agreed structure and is dominated by the Deutschmark. Crises are resolved by periodic re- and de-valuations in Brussels.

Appendix II: The Institutions of the EEC

ECU: The European Currency Unit in which the combination of the EMS currencies is expressed. Has acquired some status as a form of exchange. Its physical existence is theoretical, beyond a 100-ECU coin recently issued (as legal tender) by the Belgian government. Some countries permit private accounts to be held in ECU.

EUA: The European Unit of Account. Lowly cousin of the ECU. An internal accounting measure used by the institutions of the EEC, over-riding the twelve member states' currencies, to do the household sums.

MCAs: Monetary compensation amounts. Border taxes for agricultural imports and exports. Grit in the system and contrary to the purity of a genuine common market.

BIBLIOGRAPHY

The Politics of Agriculture in the European Community, Edmund Neville-Rolfe, Policy Studies Institute, London.

The World Food Problem, David Grigg, Basil Blackwell, Oxford.

Agriculture: the triumph and the shame, Richard Body, Temple Smith, London.

Ireland in Crisis, Raymond Crotty, Brandon, County Kerry, Ireland.

The Political Economy of International Agricultural Policy, Geoff Millar, Australian Government, Canberra.

Common Ground, Adrian Moyes, Oxfam, Oxford.

EC Structures Policy and UK Agriculture, B. J. Revell, Centre for Agricultural Strategy, Reading University.

World Development Report, 1986, the World Bank.

20th General Report on Activities of the European Communities, European Commission, Brussels.

The EC Common Agricultural Policy and the Environment, Dolf Logemann, Stichting Natuur en Milieu, Utrecht.

Nitrates in Food and Water, Her Majesty's Stationery Office, London.

Socio-structural Policy in Agriculture, House of Lords select committee on EEC, Her Majesty's Stationery Office, London.

Silent Spring, Rachel Carson, Penguin, London.

Farming and Rural Enterprise, Her Majesty's Stationery Office, London.

Multitudinous reports and conclusions of the European Parliament.

INDEX

Index

Index

Hord, Brian 106
Howe, Sir Geoffrey 122

Independent, The 119
Institute of Policy Studies,
Washington 143
InterAgra 54
International Food Exhibition,
London 18
Intervention Board for Agricultural
Produce 67
Ireland
  barley export swindle 102
  deleterious effect of CAP
  membership 146–51 *passim*
  economic crisis 145, 146, 147
  emigration 145–6
  European Movement 151
  farming 147, 149–50
  farming debt 148, 149, 150
  joins EEC, 1973 147
  joins EMS 101, 149
  national debt 145
  overvalued punt 147–8
  pork carousel swindle 102–3
  potato's role 152–3
  problems of 'green punt' 40
  reasons for joining EEC 148, 153
  Squeeze on industrial workers
  148–9
  Third World status 152, 153
  Ulster border smuggling swindle
  100
Italy 105
  butter-go-round swindle 99–100
  Mafia frauds on CAP 106–10 *passim*,
  179
  meat fraud 104
  olive oil fraud 106–7, 109
  tomato fraud 107

Jagan, Cheddi 90
Jamaica
  illegal exports of marijuana 96
  sugar exports 97
  sugar jobs lost 97
  turbulent economy 90, 96
Japan 116, 174
  long-term economic plan 114
  Pacific as dependency of 135
  protectionism 124
  R & D spending 174

trade wars with EEC 123–5
  vulnerable agriculture 125
Jenkins, Roy 21, 27
  head of European Commission 19,
  20
  support for CAP 19
Jenkins, Simon 169
Jopling, Michael 16, 18, 23, 26, 30, 35,
46, 56, 57, 126, 127, 164, 166
  attacked by NFU 23, 29, 75, 165,
  166
  plans for 'alternative' rural strategy
  75–6, 165, 166

Kenya: unwanted food aid, 1983 141
Kiechle, Ignaz 24, 26, 31, 45, 70
Kissinger, Henry 128

Labour Party 115, 117
Lomé Convention 92, 97
  EEC's poor deal for signatories
  137–8

MacGregor, John: double-think on
CAP 45, 46, 47
Malaysia 135
Manley, Norman 90
Mansholt, Dr Sicco 14, 15, 32, 74, 158,
167
  architect of CAP 32–5 *passim*, 38,
  39, 40, 57, 72, 181
  on CAP today 47–9
  proposals to cut food production,
  1968 41–2
Marshall Plan 33, 143
Mergers and Monopolies
Commission 94, 95
Milk
  attempt to cut production, 1986–7
  56–7
  CAP price 162
  dried milk mountain 50, 64
  European herd of cows 50
  milk quotas, 1984 55, 56
Milk Marketing Board 57, 59–64, 177
  'Dairy Crest' subsidiary 63
  'doorstep pinta' 60–1, 62
  EEC disapproval 59–61
  high price of milk 61, 62, 63
  monthly milk cheque for farmers 60
Miller, Geoffrey 126
Ministry of Agriculture 156

Index

conflict with Dept. of Environment over land policy 76, 156, 163–7
suppression of research on pollution 158
Mitterrand, Pres. François 49
Monde, Le 119
Monkton, Christopher 21
Montague, Michael 58

National Consumer Council 58
National Farmers Union (NFU) 23, 44, 72, 156, 165
conference, 1987 23, 29, 75, 165, 166
opposition to milk quotas, 1984 56
support for food quotas 58–9
National Health Service 88
New Zealand 18
effect of abandonment of agricultural subsidies 127–8
North Atlantic Treaty Organisation (NATO) 118

Owen, Dr David 71, 72
Oxfam 141, 142
Oxford Farming Conference, 1987 45, 67

Patten, Chris 141
Pearce, Andrew 54
Plumb, Henry 56
Pompidou, President 42, 43
Pooley, Peter 36–7, 125, 168, 178
condemns Greek raisins 85–6
on CAP 37, 38, 51
Price, Peter 28, 172

Rapeseed oil 121
Reagan, Pres. Ronald 119
Ridley, Nicholas 163–6 *passim*
Roberts, Sir Stephen 62
Rocard, Michel 22, 56

Saudi Arabia: green revolution 174
Seaga, Edward 96
Sheehy, Prof. 149, 150, 151
Siamwalla, Prof. Amma 133
Somalia: waste of food aid 140
Spedding, Prof. Colin 75, 161, 180
Star 50
Strauss, Franz-Josef 42
Sudan: waste of food aid 140
Sugar 87, 179

beet farmers 89, 90, 93–4
Caribbean 89, 96–7
cost of transporting unwanted 138
depressed price, 1986–7 88, 96
EEC excess production 92, 138
slackening of demand 87
sugar-cane countries 87, 89
sugar pronounced unhealthy 88
Swift, Jonathan 15

Tate & Lyle 89, 91
effect of UK joining EEC on 92–5 *passim*
fights off nationalisation 90
sugar monopoly 90
take-over bid for British Sugar 94, 95
Taylor, Teddy 50, 164
'European Reform Group' 115
Thailand
EEC compensation cheque 135
tapioca crisis 132–4
Thatcher, Margaret 20, 21, 26, 61, 74, 115, 117, 164, 165
attacks NFU 23
British EEC contribution and 20–1, 27
Tiedemann, Prof. Klaus 98, 111
Times, The 94
Togo: insufficient food aid 140
Treaty of Rome 11–16 *passim*, 24, 33, 78, 89, 183
article 39 on CAP 32, 34, 35, 47, 82
thirtieth anniversary, 1987 171

Unilever 122
Union of Soviet Socialist Republics (USSR) 116
agricultural improvement, late 1980s 174
exploitation of EEC surpluses 52, 70
harvests, 1986 and 1987 70, 173
need for US grain 139
possibility of reaching grain self-sufficiency 173–4
United Kingdom
agri-millionaires 161, 162
ALURE (Alternative Land Use for the Rural Economy) policy 76, 163–6 *passim*, 178, 180
butter hand-outs, 1987 58
cane-sugar quota 92–3

191